BROKEN BOW'S BLACK COMMUNITIES AND DUNBAR HIGH SCHOOL

A Glimpse into the Past from a Black Perspective

BROKEN BOW'S BLACK COMMUNITIES AND DUNBAR HIGH SCHOOL

A Glimpse into the Past from a Black Perspective

BY DR. SIDNEY CARTER

Oklahoma Horizons Series

Copyright 2011 by Oklahoma Heritage Association
All rights reserved. No part of this book may be reproduced or utilized in any form by means electronic or mechanical, including photocopying and recording, by any information storage and retrieval system, without permission of Oklahoma Heritage Association.
Printed in Canada

ISBN: 978-1-885596-93-2

Library of Congress Control Number: 2011930385

Designed by Kris Vculek

OKLAHOMA HERITAGE | Association

CHAIRMAN
Calvin Anthony
Stillwater

CHAIRMAN ELECT
Kathy Taylor
Tulsa

CHAIRMAN EMERITUS
Tom J. McDaniel
Oklahoma City

PRESIDENT
Shannon L. Rich
Oklahoma City

VICE CHAIRMEN
Bill Anoatubby
Ada

Bill Burgess
Lawton

Ike Glass
Newkirk

Jane Jayroe Gamble
Oklahoma City

Fred Harlan
Okmulgee

David Kyle
Tulsa

John Massey
Durant

Stan Clark
Stillwater

AT LARGE EXECUTIVE COMMITTEE MEMBERS
Clayton I. Bennett
Oklahoma City

Bond Payne
Oklahoma City

Glen D. Johnson
Oklahoma City

CORPORATE SECRETARY
Mark A. Stansberry
Edmond

TREASURER
Nevyle Cable
Okmulgee

CHAIRMEN'S CIRCLE
Pat Henry
Lawton

Roxana Lorton
Tulsa

J.W. McLean
Dallas, TX

Lee Allan Smith
Oklahoma City

G. Lee Stidham
Checotah

DIRECTORS
Alison Anthony
Tulsa

Howard Barnett
Tulsa

Barbara Braught
Duncan

Joe Cappy
Tulsa

Michael A. Cawley
Ardmore

Paul Cornell
Bristow

Carol Crawford
Frederick

Rebecca Dixon
Tulsa

Ford Drummond
Bartlesville

Patti Evans
Ponca City

Christy Everest
Oklahoma City

Vaughndean Fuller
Tulsa

Gilbert "Gib" Gibson
Lawton

Dan Gilliam
Bartlesville

Jim Halsey
Tulsa

Jean Harbison
Lawton

V. Burns Hargis
Stillwater

George Henderson
Norman

Robert Henry
Oklahoma City

Duke R. Ligon
Oklahoma City

Vicki Miles-LaGrange
Oklahoma City

Joe Moran
Tulsa

Melvin Moran
Seminole

Fred Morgan
Oklahoma City

C.D. Northcutt
Ponca City

Gary D. Parker
Muskogee

Gregory E. Pyle
Durant

Carl Renfro
Ponca City

Frank C. Robson
Claremore

Richard N. Ryerson
Alva

Sharon Shoulders
Henryetta

Stan Stamper
Hugo

Clayton Taylor
Oklahoma City

Steve Taylor
McAlester

Chuck Thompson
Norman

Steve Turnbo
Tulsa

Ty Tyler
Oklahoma City

Hardy Watkins
Oklahoma City

Ron White
Oklahoma City

Dedication

This book is dedicated to the courageous individuals of Broken Bow and Dunbar High School students who gallantly served in the Armed Forces of the United States of America during World War II, Korean, and Vietnam Wars. Whether voluntarily or drafted, when called to duty, these individuals bravely stepped up and fulfilled their military obligation to their country.

Due to a limited ability in researching, the author realizes that the list below is not all inclusive, therefore, an apology is given in advance for any omissions; however, to all who served, and to some who gave their lives, the city of Broken Bow, the State of Oklahoma and the Country owe you and your family a debt of gratitude. God Bless each of you who served.

PARTIAL LISTING

WORLD WAR II • 1939-1945

Willie Jordan, Sr	Clifford Carter	James Caldwell
Sedalia Carter	Clarence Burris	Charles H. Butler
James Burris	Rastus Burris	Credell Westbrook
Hickman Burris	Curtis Cantley	Dunnie Harris
Dellie Hawthorne	Martin Lewis	Robert Burris

KOREA • 1950-1953

Ivory Lee Butler, Jr.
Andrew Colbert
Manuel Colbert
Donald Burris
Charles Burris
L.D. Lewis
Bill Hamilton
Walter Lewis
Herman Carter

C. J. Pennington, Jr.
Jackie Garrett
Edward L. Garrett
Wilbur D. Garrett
Ruben Duckett
Ike Maddock
Elmer Maddock
Arma G. Wiseman
G.B. Burris
James Sykes

Eddie Sykes
Jimmy Lee Love
M. C. Richards
Elijah Burris
Cedell Hill
Cleon Hill
Lennon Sykes
Clarence Radford
Willie Lewis

VIETNAM • 1955-1975

Vernell Ramsey
Clarence Lewis
Walter Wheeler
Billy J. Kellum
Willie L. Frazier, Jr.
Larry Taylor
James E. Carter
Theodis Kennybrew
President Carter, Jr.
Larry Williams

Sidney Carter, Sr.
Lonnie Johnson
John Jordan
Emmitt Bizzell, Jr.
Clark G. Warren
LeVan Williams
Ralph Bizzell
Chonkie Duckett
Harold Duckett

Clifford Duckett
Bernice Hackett
Paul Richards
Charles Lewis, Jr.
Winzell Hamilton
Webster Wheeler, Jr.
Adell Lewis, Jr.
Charlie Burris
Isaiah Lewis

CONTENTS

ACKNOWLEDGMENTS 9

INTRODUCTION 11

BROKEN BOW'S GROWTH 12

BROKEN BOW'S DEMOGRAPHICS 13

BROKEN BOW'S ECONOMY 13

GOVERNANCE 14

CHAPTER 1
EARLY HISTORY 15

CHAPTER 2
FAMILY LIFE 18

CHAPTER 3
LEISURE TIME 25

CHAPTER 4
BLACK COMMUNITIES AND THEIR CITIZENS 32

CHAPTER 5
CHURCHES 48

CHAPTER 6
ENTREPRENEURS/ SUCCESSFUL DUNBAR GRADS 52

CHAPTER 7
THE SCHOOLS 62

CHAPTER 8
SPORTS 140

SCHOOL SONG 151

SUMMARY 153

BIBLIOGRAPHY 155

INDEX 156

Broken Bow's first school for blacks, established in the early 1880s, was located in Pleasant Valley, however at the time of publication no photo was available.

Dunbar High School, built in 1934.

The last Dunbar High School shortly after completion, 1954 -1955.

Acknowledgments

Capturing the history of one's town, its citizens, and its school is a difficult task. It is virtually impossible to cover every fact, every individual, or event in its entirety; consequently there are some omissions. The author realizes there will be critics who will say "why wasn't this or that" included in the book. To everyone who reads this book, be assured that a sincere attempt has been made to be as inclusive as possible. While information on some black citizens of Broken Bow was more accessible than others, extreme care was taken to ensure that no single individual or family was excessively spotlighted, profiled, or emphasized.

The primary purpose for writing the book was to preserve some of our history, and to leave a memorable legacy to those of us still alive, as well as to our children and grandchildren who may read this book twenty or thirty years in the future. It is the author's hope that the primary purpose will supersede any criticism.

Writing a book is a long, tiring, and tedious pursuit. You start with excitement, with a vision, and a deep desire to write something you feel is important, needed, and will be viewed by others with your same passion. In the process you come to realize that writing is a lonely endeavor; it's sometimes frustrating, and research is time consuming. The journey dictates dedication and tenacity to continue writing when you doubt if it is all really worthwhile. It requires that you take valuable time from your family and those you care most about. I experienced all of these emotions as I wrote.

Consequently, it is with sincere thanks that I express my gratitude to all those who aided in writing this book. The Oklahoma Historical Society's *Encyclopedia of Oklahoma History and Culture*, numerous Broken Bow citizens, and Dunbar graduates provided invaluable information for parts of the history included in the book.

I am extremely indebted to President Carter, Jr. who permitted me to frequently burn his ears, often times as early as three, four, or five o'clock in the morning for hours as we discussed the book.

I also would like to personally express sincere appreciation to my family, particularly my wife Barbara, who supported me as I stole numerous hours of family time locked away writing, and to my children, Lakisha, Sidney, Jr., Steve, and Mark who encouraged me to continue writing when I wanted to quit.

I hope the book captures some of the toils and celebrations that I, as well as other black citizens, experienced while growing up and living in the town of Broken Bow.

—Sidney Carter

Introduction

The land that would become Broken Bow was owned by the Choctaw Tribe prior to being settled by non- Indians. Located at the junction of United States Highways 70 and 259, the City of Broken Bow was founded in 1910. The town was incorporated and a post office established on September 23, 1911. Although Broken Bow was located on land previously owned by the Choctaws, it did not receive its name from its local American Indian roots. It was named after Broken Bow, Nebraska, the hometown of Herman and Hans Dierks, who moved to southeastern Oklahoma to establish the Choctaw Lumber Company.

This small southeastern Oklahoma town in McCurtain County, nestled in the foothills of the Kiamichi Mountains, was almost named "Con Chito", after a small Indian village that existed in 1910 at the time Broken Bow was incorporated. Faith, however, deemed otherwise and due to Herman and Hans Dierks, the town was named "Broken Bow". The area platted for Broken Bow was at the eastern terminus of the Texas, Oklahoma and Eastern Railroad. The land on north of side of the tracks was designated for residences, schools, churches, and retailers. The land south of the tracks was reserved for the lumber mill, employee housing, and other parts of the Choctaw Lumber Company. The firm provided a doctor for its workers and their families and built a hospital chiefly for the company employees but open to anyone needing care.

Early settlers of this Little Dixie region were primarily Southerners seeking a new start following the American Civil War.

Growth

By 1920 the city had grown to a population of 1,983, and by 1923 Broken Bow enjoyed a public water and sewage system and had electric lighting. Five churches, two elementary schools, a high school for whites, a separate school for blacks, and thirty-two businesses were established. The town also boasted three lawyers, two dentists, and five physicians. The population of Broken Bow has shown a steady increase from 1,983 in 1920 to 4,230 in 2000 except for a 7.77 percent decline between 1940 and 1950. The population of Broken Bow in 1990 was 3,961 residents. It is anticipated that the 2010 census will show a considerable increase.

Choctaw Chief Jefferson Gardner's home near Broken Bow. Built in 1884, the home has been preserved since 1910 by three generations of the Stiles Family.

Demographics

As of the 2000 census, racial makeup of the city was 64.23% White, 9.43% African American, 17.80% Native American, 0.19% Asian, 0.05% Pacific Islander, 2.06% from other races, and 6.24% from two or more races. Hispanic or Latino of any race was 5.32% of the population. The median income for a household in the city was $18,068, and the median income for a family was $20,676. Males had a median income of $20,398 versus $17,155 for females. The per capita income for the city was $10,028. About 34.8% of families and 38.9% of the population were below the poverty line, including 52.2% of those under the age of 18 and 22.7% age 65 or over.

Economy

At the beginning of the twenty-first century, timber remained the economic base of Broken Bow. The Dierks brothers sold their holdings in Oklahoma and Arkansas to the Weyerhaeuser Company in late 1969. Included in this sale was the Broken Bow mill, then one of the largest lumber mills in the nation. Another important business in the area is Tyson Industries' chicken-processing plant. Originally established by Lane Industry in 1970, the Broken Bow plant currently processes an average of one-million birds per week.

The tourism industry is also an integral part of the local economy. Twelve miles north of Broken Bow is Beavers Bend State Park and Resort. More than 1.3 million visitors per year take advantage of the superb recreational facilities offered around the parks Broken Bow Lake created on the Mountain Fork River by the United States Corps of Engineers in the 1960s. Hochatown State Park and Cedar Creek Golf Course also are in the Beavers Bend area.

Because of the rich variety of game and wildlife in the area, sportsmen inundate the region. Hunters from near and far make frequent trips to this region of McCurtain County to fish and hunt. Because of the plethora of deer in the area, the region has been marketed as the "deer capital of the world".

Governance

Currently the city of Broken Bow operates under a Statutory Council-Manager form of government. The council consists of four council members and one mayor. Four members are elected from their wards and one is elected at-large.

Throughout the history of the council, two black citizens, Garfield Johnson and Ray Burris, have served as members representing Ward 1. Ray Burris is currently a member of the council and has served for 14 years.

Chapter 1
EARLY HISTORY

It is with great pleasure and fond memories of Broken Bow that this book is written. The scope of this book is intended to recapture or expound some of the early history, experiences, and lives of selected black citizens and families of Broken Bow prior to integration of the schools. A rich and storied history, immersed in segregation, is embedded in this quaint southeastern Oklahoma town in McCurtain County.

The book's primary focus centers on the time period of Broken Bow's incorporation through 1965. Certainly not all inclusive, but brief snippets of Broken Bow's black citizens and the communities they lived in are narrated. Many of the complete details surrounding the black communities in Broken Bow have been lost because few written records were kept. As a result, capturing much of the town's history proved to be extremely illusive. Personal interviews would have provided firsthand testimonies or factual insight as to dates, events, times, and places for this writing; unfortunately, most of those who could provide such data have long since deceased. Consequently, as a native of Broken Bow, the author has relied heavily upon his memory and personal experiences, some prior research, anecdotal information, and undocumented occurrences to describe the history of the black communities of Broken Bow, "*a place he loves and still calls home*".

Although some of the anecdotal events expressed in this writing may seem unjust to the current day reader, the book is by no means intended to be an indictment on the town of Broken Bow or its white citizens. It is simply intended to characterize life as it was for the black citizens of Broken Bow during the early years. To paraphrase a quote from scripture; "all it takes for injustice to prosper is for good men to say or do nothing". Perhaps this writing will ensure that one Broken Bow citizen is not guilty of such a quote and has spoken out.

Obviously, in Broken Bow between the years of 1930 and 1940, e-mail, twitter, and facebook had not emerged. Communication was done primarily by letters or word of mouth. Prior research indicates the first telephone company in Broken Bow was established during the year 1911 by the Callaham family. Few black families, if any, had a phone at this time. A family's cost to rent a single residential phone was approximately $1.65 per month and those families who could afford it were assigned a party line. Several individuals would be assigned to the same party line and conversations were never private.

Phone numbers were not assigned. In order to contact another person, the calling party would initiate various combinations of cranks such as one long and two short cranks or maybe three long cranks. Oftentimes individuals would have to wait for hours to secure a line because it seemed that someone else was always on the line when you needed to use the phone. Every once in a while one could eavesdrop or cut in on someone else's conversation. Needless to say, the party line created many conflicts among telephone users.

Most black residents readily recognize the names of Ortho Morren and Bertie Creed, long time telephone operators in Broken Bow who were responsible for connecting parties when a call had to be made.

Prior research documents that by 1921 the business section of the city of Broken Bow and adjacent residential areas had limited electricity, a sewer system, and running water. However, outlying communities such as Pleasant Valley and Lukfata still had outhouses for toilets and used kerosene lamps for lighting.

A Magneto Crank Telephone similar to those available in the early 1900s. Courtesy Wikipedia Free Encyclopedia.

Chapter 2
FAMILY LIFE

During the early years the makeup of most black families in Broken Bow consisted of both parents in the home. In many instances childbirth was accomplished with the aid of a midwife. Noted black midwives of the time were Berda White, Aunt Verdie, Roberta Burris, and Addie Carson. Though seldom used, most black families used home remedies to treat illnesses, familiar doctors during this time were Dr. Dobney, Dr. Shuford, Dr. Chastain, and Dr. C. T. McDonald. Later, Dr. Sherrill, Dr. Baker, and G. C. Mullins practiced medicine in the city. More recent doctors would include Dr. Roark, Dr. Whittaker and Dr. Harold Chandler. All the doctors were white men as there were no black doctors in the city of Broken Bow during this period.

Black families were generally large, five or six children and a few with as many as ten or twelve, living on small acreages or plots of land where they planted large gardens to provide vegetables. Most acquired meat for the family by raising cattle, chickens, and pigs.

Every family member pulled his or her own weight and had specific chores that had to be accomplished each day. In most homes, wood burning stoves were used for warmth and cooking; therefore, some member of the family had to get up early each morning and fire up the stoves. Children had to "slop the pigs" and "feed the chickens" each morning before going to school. Because most homes did not have running water, someone had to draw fresh water from the well or spring for drinking and washing dishes. Life was really "a family affair" and it took each member's contribution to make certain the family survived and their needs were met.

Moms canned apples, peaches, blackberries, tomatoes, okra, squash, cabbage, turnips, corn, and made plum jelly to ensure the family had plenty of vegetables and the like for winter. Fathers killed pigs or cattle and cured meat for the family. Almost everyone had a "smokehouse" where meat would be salted and preserved for later use. Some dad's hunted quail or trapped squirrels and rabbits for meat.

A great Sunday meal would consist of mashed potatoes, greens, pinto beans or black eyed peas, chicken, cornbread, iced tea, and some sort of dessert, such as pound cake or banana pudding. That's what was called "good eating."

Regarding food, clothing, or other material possessions, a common saying by many black families was, "we may not have had a lot but we always had enough".

Not much was wasted in the black family and a creed that most lived by was "use it up, wear it out, make it do, or do without". Families also shared what they had with their neighbors. Whether digging a well, bailing hay, slaughtering hogs, or picking vegetables from the garden, neighbors worked together and shared the bounty.

Youth could earn money doing odd jobs such as bailing hay for two cents a bail, clearing land, digging wells, or simply picking up pop bottles and carrying them to the nearest store where you could receive a two- or three-cent

In 1946 President Carter, Sr. purchased a home and five acres in Pleasant Valley for $500.

deposit for each bottle.

James Edward Carter worked for Riley Moore, a local insurance agent, clearing land on his property. Kenneth Broussard and President Carter, Jr. worked killing and dressing out hogs for Mr. Whitten and Mr. Pace who operated slaughter houses. Bernice Hackett lived with and was a driver for Joe Hough as he traveled about buying and selling cattle. Val Gene and Charlie Golston performed the job of mopping the floors and cleaning Chandler Hewitt's drugstore several times each week. After Val Gene and Charlie graduated and left Broken Bow, Willie L. Jordan, Jr., John Jordan, and Michel Jordan respectively performed these duties at the drugstore. Willie "W.L." Lewis worked for Jack Lane at the Ford Motor Company detailing cars.

In the black communities, doors were seldom locked when leaving homes. During the heat of the summer months, because most homes were without air conditioning, it was common to sleep at night with the windows open and only the screen doors closed. When the temperature peaked, 100 to 102 degrees, it was common to sleep outside at night on a cot under a tree.

This trusting attitude might seem strange because history records that the town of Broken Bow was born during an epidemic of killings; particularly in the white communities. In stark contrast to the white communities, except for a few minor infractions, such as stealing watermelons out of someone's watermelon patch and taking pears off someone's pear tree, crime or misbehavior almost was nonexistent in the black communities of Broken Bow.

Previous research has reported that during the early years in the white communities of the town of Broken Bow it was not uncommon to have murders almost weekly. Writings from early research history have reported that from statehood in 1907 to 1920, McCurtain County had more than 500 murders. Very few of these murders involved black citizens. Perhaps the killings could be attributed to the county's location which made it attractive and a relatively safe haven for law breaking individuals who migrated to Broken Bow from bordering states.

Misbehavior in the black community simply was not tolerated. If a youth did anything at school that required discipline, the details of the incident generally were known by their parents before the child arrived home from school at which time most parents administered a second dose of discipline to demonstrate their support of the school. If and when the youth went to church, the pastor also knew of the misdeeds he or she may have perpetrated and were righteously admonished. The parents, the school, and the church spoke as a single unit during the early years.

It was common for a neighboring parent to paddle a child for any misbehavior he or she might commit in their presence. The neighbor would then report the incident to the child's biological parents who would administer a second paddling. The unity among black citizens and the various families is best illustrated in the following scenario as told by a citizen of Broken Bow:

A father had to go out of town on personal business. This well respected father had to be gone for several days. While he was away, one of his sons got into a bit of

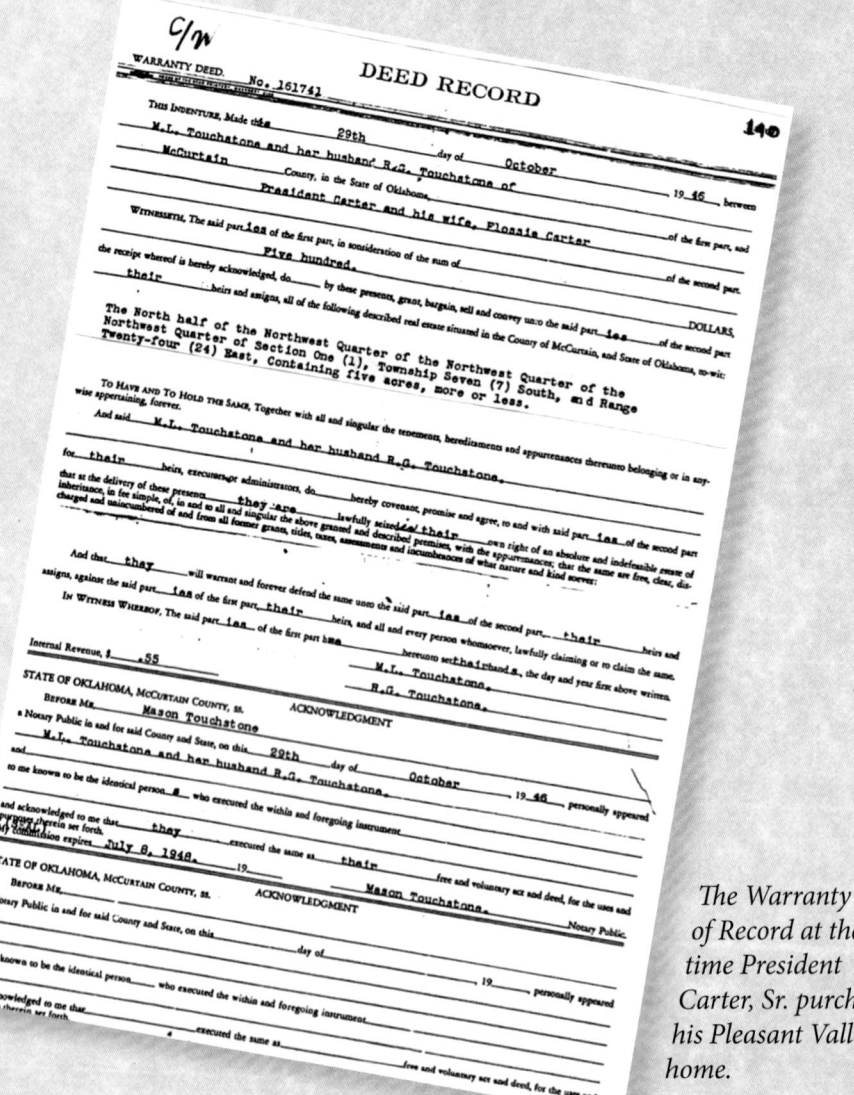

The Warranty Deed of Record at the time President Carter, Sr. purchased his Pleasant Valley home.

mischief. A neighboring father reported the incident to the father who was out of town. His response to the neighboring father was "you whipped his a_ _ didn't you? Thanks, for letting me know, and of course, I will take care of this issue when I return."

When laws were broken and a citizen got into trouble the city of Broken Bow and McCurtain County had elected sheriffs to maintain order in the area. Early county sheriffs included Gene Harris, Walter Irons, Joe Hough, Clarence Lane, Tee Bo Jones, and Don Skeens. Joe Hough is the only McCurtain County sheriff to have served three consecutive terms. Noted deputies who served with these sheriffs are Snowball Stewart, Elzie Lee King, and Larkin Wimbley.

Even though Elzie King was deputized, being black, his authority was somewhat limited and he was deputized to maintain order primarily among those within his community. His authority was very limited in the white community.

On several occasions President Carter, Sr., who was light skinned, was picked up and taken to the Broken Bow City Hall to be arrested because the deputies who picked him up did not know he was black. They would report, "we picked up this white man who was hanging around down in the Colored Quarters". Gene Harris or Walter Irons would immediately inform them, "Let that man go, that's President Carter, Sr. and he and his family live in the Quarters."

Nothing angered President Carter, Sr. more than to be mistaken as a white person, or to be called a "peckerwood". If you wanted to get him riled up, call him a white man. Dierks Lumber Company authorities forced President Carter, Sr. and his family to move out of the Quarters alleging that he was selling bootleg whiskey.

In 1946 President Carter, Sr. moved his family from the Quarters to Pleasant Valley. He purchased five acres of land and the home from M. L. and R. G. Touchstone for $500. President Carter, Sr. became a successful entrepreneur and made a living selling bootleg whiskey, farming, trapping various games, hunting, fishing, and selling squirrels and rabbits to support his family. The Carter family maintained ownership of the home and property in Pleasant Valley until 1989 at which time it was sold to Curtis Cantley. Curtis Cantley had the home torn down and later sold the property to Julius Lewis.

Chapter 3
LEISURE TIME

Most black adults spent leisure time hunting, fishing, playing cards, checkers, or dominoes under their favorite shade tree. Adults also spent many hours just sitting on their porches discussing matters of the time. Of course kids were never permitted to hang around during these discussions. This was grown-up talk and kids were shooed away and admonished to go somewhere else and play.

Youth spent their leisure time playing hopscotch, stick ball, blind man bluff, or skinny dipping in the nearest creek. Oftentimes in Pleasant Valley and Lukfata the nearest neighbor was ¼ mile or farther away. As a result, kids were forced to invent their own games and play with their siblings. Long days were spent in open fields catching June Bugs, playing catch with a rag ball, baseball, football, or shooting an old basketball into a makeshift goal if you could keep the basketball aired up. Kids played cowboys and Indians, rode stick horses, and made tong walkers out of tin cans.

It always was fun to play hide and go seek, especially as it began to get dark.

Early on in the Quarters, baseball was a popular pastime for families. On Sunday afternoons black teams from surrounding areas would come to Broken Bow to play baseball games. Jack Brewer managed the Broken Bow team and had fairly good players in Sam Young, Jr., Johnnie B. Carter, Homer Gordon, Willie L. Sykes, Genie Cubit, A. Z. Cunts, Clifford Carter, and Herman Carter, among others.

In the early days, battery-operated radios provided most electronic entertainment because there were few televisions in the homes of black families. If a family was fortunate enough to have a television, it was common for five or six kids to gather in that home each day or night, sprawl out on the floor, and watch their favorite programs.

Some of the favorite early programs were *Playhouse 90, The Ed Sullivan Show, Gunsmoke, Highway Patrol, Have Gun Will Travel, Dragnet, Superman, 77 Sunset Strip, Amos 'n' Andy, I Love Lucy, Alfred Hitchcock Presents, The Twilight Zone, $64,000 Question, American Bandstand, The Little Rascals, The General Electric Hour*, and, of course, Friday night wrestling.

Travel primarily was done by walking, using a wagon with a team of mules, or maybe riding the family pony. If you were affluent enough to own a vehicle, gas was 17 cents per gallon for Regular and 25 cents for Ethel.

The uptown movie house was a favorite hangout for black youth, particularly during the hot summer months because the building was air conditioned. Black youth would see a show at the Chief Theater if they could obtain the 25 cents admission. A popular activity on Saturday nights, of course with your parents' permission, was to watch the first show and then stay late for the second movie called the "preview", a showing of the upcoming week's movie. Blacks were not allowed to sit in the downstairs section of the movie theater; they sat in the balcony of the movie house where the projection room was located.

Black citizens were not permitted to go into the local pool hall, located next door to the Chief Theater. If blacks desired to eat while in town they could go up a set of stairs into the back entrance of the Gems' Café, the kitchen, where they could purchase and be served a meal on a butcher-block table or get a hamburger "to go" wrapped in cellophane paper and handed to them in a brown paper bag. The practice was similar at the local Dairy Queen and Crouse's Dairy Freeze drive-ins. Blacks could not go inside these facilities, but ordered their food from a small window opening. Waitresses were generally polite. However, many establishments displayed a very visible sign that read "we reserve the right to refuse service to anyone".

The irony is, while blacks were not permitted to go inside or eat inside these facilities, in many cases the food being served had been prepared by black cooks. In many private homes, black maids prepared the food. One cannot concretely know the rationale for such regulations, but causes one to ponder: Did whites really not want to eat with blacks? Was it to ensure that blacks and whites did not socialize?

Chandler Hewitt and Sherrill's drugstores did permit blacks to purchase fountain drinks inside their stores, but they were not allowed to sit at tables or in booths and read comic magazines. They had to purchase their orders to go. It was commonplace to see restroom facilities and drinking fountains that displayed signs that read "whites only" or "coloreds only".

Unjust as these events may seem; hardly ever was opposition to the rules displayed. Blacks simply understood that this was the way of life in their segregated hometown. Black parents regularly reminded their children, "you stay in your place and you will stay out of trouble."

A widely observed celebration, particularly in the southern states, was the 19th of June. "Juneteenth" as it was called was a known celebration commemorating the end of slavery in the United States. According to *TIME* Magazine, it was on June 19th in 1865 that the Union soldiers, led by Major General Gordon Granger, landed at Galveston, Texas, with news that the Civil War had ended and that the enslaved were free. This came almost two years after President Abraham Lincoln's Emancipation Proclamation. Consequently, the nineteenth of June commemorated Independence Day for black citizens during this period. Broken Bow's black citizens, like many other black communities, looked forward to this date as it was the start of a four-day celebration. The event usually began on Thursday morning and ran through Sunday.

Dierks Lumber Company in Broken Bow wholeheartedly supported the event and permitted black workers to take off for the four-day celebration. Dierks provided meat for barbecuing and built a huge platform to serve as a dance floor. The event was joyous and members from all four Communities—Quarters, New Addition, Pleasant Valley, and Lukfata—took part in the celebration.

Oftentimes black Broken Bow citizens who had migrated to other cities and states would return to participate in the Juneteenth festivities in Broken Bow. The miraculous part is even with the frolicking, drinking, and merrymaking few, if any, incidents or infractions of the law occurred.

Phil Savage, Jake Butler, Cleve Dallas, W. C. Butler, Sam Young, Sr., and Willie Mae Cole, among others, usually built huge barbecue pits and were known to make some of the best pork, beef, chicken, and goat barbecue sandwiches in town. They each created their own special sauces, either hot or mild depending upon your taste. Rather than a brush, they used a stick with a rag on the end to create a mop like instrument to splash on the tasty sauces. Competition was intense as the best sauce was considered the key ingredient in making a sandwich unique. Nothing was better than a good barbecue sandwich and an orange or strawberry soda pop.

White vendors set up booths for taking photos at a cost of 25 cents. Other booths were available and for a price you could take a chance on winning some sort of prize by spinning a wheel or throwing a baseball to knock down rag like figures. These booths always were present giving the event a carnival-like atmosphere.

Dance competitions always were a part of the celebration. James Edward Broussard, Lilly May Young, and Big Boy King were very good dancers. Excitement always was created as the audience watched and expressed their opinions as to who performed best.

Few, if any, whites, other than the vendors, appeared at these celebrations. The county sheriff would occasionally drive through to ensure the festivities were peaceful. During one celebration, a white gentleman, reportedly from California, who obviously did not harbor any prejudices about mingling with blacks, came and stole the show with his dancing talents. Each day of the event, he and Mary Neal James mesmerized the crowd with their jitterbug steps as they danced to the musical tune of "In the Mood".

Today, recognition of Juneteenth as a holiday varies from state to state. With many blacks having moved from rural to urban cities, interest in celebrating the event has vacillated from high to low over the years. In 2011, 36 states recognized the event as a holiday.

Another popular event sponsored by the city of Broken Bow was an Annual Rodeo. The first rodeo was sponsored in July, 1946 by American Legion Post 297. It was held in the Memorial Football Stadium and, tragically, 16-year-old competitor Hardy Whatley, Jr. of Bethel was killed when the bull he was riding trampled him to death. An attempt was made to save the young boy's life when County Sheriff Clarence Lane rushed the boy to the hospital in DeQueen, Arkansas.

In later years, the Jaycees sponsored the rodeo and black residents were permitted to attend and enjoy. Famed cowboy and rodeo producer Jim Shoulders provided excellent bucking stock, bulls and horses, for the rodeo.

During one rodeo, Willie "W. L." Lewis, who worked at the Lane's Motor Company, entered the competition to ride a bull on a "dare" from some of his white co-workers. Willie rode one jump out of the shoot before being bucked off. This episode is how Willie earned the nickname "Cowboy".

Oftentimes on Saturday night, the last day of the event, the rodeo would include a street dance in the heart of Broken Bow. Cowgirls and cowboys dressed in their expensive rhinestone western outfits would "boot scoot" the night away. Main Street would be blocked off to ensure the safety of the participants. The street dances always had a country and western band to provide the music; consequently, few blacks, if any, participated in the dancing. Truth is, it was not clearly understood whether blacks were allowed to participate. This was one of those situations where there were no written rules; as a black, you simply stayed in your place so as to "not rock the boat".

Chapter 4
BLACK COMMUNITIES AND THEIR CITIZENS

Black citizens in the town of Broken Bow resided primarily in four communities. Initially, early black residents resided in a sector of town south of the city and just east of the Choctaw Mill called the "Pasture". According to Earnestine Cherry, the Pasture consisted of a small number of rent houses and a boarding house. The entire complex was surrounded by barbed-wire fencing. Cherry remembered that gates to the entrance of the Pasture were locked at night and residents were kept inside the compound by armed guards until morning. This account of the Pasture is corroborated by Bob Burke in his book *Broken Bow: The First Century*. The arrangement seems to indicate that "whites" at that time were extremely fearful of blacks and felt a need to segregate, regulate, and control the movements of these citizens. The barbed wire and armed guards eerily reminded some of a concentration camp. This arrangement continued for approximately nine years, until 1920, when the Pasture was discontinued and gave birth to what became known as the Quarters.

The Quarters operated similarly, but without the barbed-wire fence and armed guards. The Quarters consisted of homes owned by Dierks Lumber Company and provided affordable housing for company workers. Monthly rent was $4.00 for a two-bedroom house and $5.00 for a three-bedroom house. Rather than an armed guard, the Quarters had what was known as a Quarter-Boss. The Quarter-Boss was an individual who walked or rode a bicycle through the Quarters each morning and evening. When talking with senior citizens in Broken Bow, they use the terms "Pasture" and "Quarters" interchangeably. Although the actual sites were the same, the two living areas operated much differently.

More affluent black citizens, such as the school teachers, resided east of Broken Bow in a sector of town called New Addition. Others populated areas three miles south of town called Pleasant Valley and west of town called Lukfata.

Certainly not inclusive, but a few prominent black family names by communities include the following:

QUARTERS

James Broussard
Phil Savage
Willie Ciscero
Jake Butler
Ms. Zeola Sykes
  (Mrs. Tee)
Willie Frazier, Sr.
Floyd Golston
Bee King
Willie Mae Cole

Clifford Duckett
Adam Lyord
Abe Gilmore
Curtis Cantley
Albert Jordan
Runion Hendricks
Cleve Dallas
Nora Westbrook
Clarence
  Pennington, Sr.

Son Dude
Ollie Miles
Henry Hollings
Bell Wilson
Taylor Elder
Rosie Cunts
Smith Hankins
Sid Smith
K. C. Jones

continued on page 34

QUARTERS *continued*

Lurene Warner
Jake Goff
Robert Elder
Emma Lee "Pig" Elder
Jack Brewer

Red Turner
Mary Lee Elder
Earl "Cripple Earl" Burris
Aaron Carter
James "Pip" Burris

Rastus "Bo Do" Burris
Earnest Richard
True Sign
Lycurgus Richard
John King

LUKFATA

Harrison Burris
Herman Butler
Charles Henry Butler
Manuel Colbert
Jake Walker
Joe David Cubit
Curtis Earnest

Austin Gable
Roosevelt "Pluck" Lewis
Tom Carter
Hickman Burris
John "Dock" Green
McCurtain Richards

L. W. Lewis, Sr.
Roman Richards
Mrs. Melissa
Alene & Frank Broussard
Charles Lewis, Sr.
Allen Meacham

PLEASANT VALLEY

Sam Hill
Ms. Lucy Ann
Jodie Burris
Roy Kennybrew
Emmitt Bizzell
Lonnie Cooper
Adell Lewis, Sr.
Ivory Butler, Sr.
Hattie Burris
William L. Richards
Clint Williams, Sr.
Clarence Reynolds
Reverend Major

President Carter, Sr.
The Maddocks
Bryant Lewis
Calvin Burris
James Allen "Bae" Green
Jessie Paxston
Otis Carson
The Ducketts
Ester Carson
Maryliza Burris
Verdie Lewis
Parker Burris

Arthel Burris
Will Hankins
Lula Arnold
Herndon Coleman
Violet Marrow
Roy Davis
Willie Rose
The Andersons
Alexander Burris
Elmo Barber
Ollie White
Martin Lewis

NEW ADDITION

Edgar Garrett
Willie Lee Jordan, Sr.
Clyde Alford
Garfield Johnson
Rosella Barr
R. M. Spigner, Sr.
H. O. Williams
G. W. Wheeler
John Givens
Roxanne Lewis
Henry Young
Chaney Polk
Sam Young, Sr.
Odelia Parks
Simon Burris
W. B. Fulsom
W. T. Holmes
Webster Wheeler, Sr.
Louise Lewis
Jewel Ramsey
L. C. and Charlie Ray Stuart
The Dickersons
Nora Radford
Patricia Releford
Neal Moses
Al Q. Hamilton
T. C. Graham
A. D. Bennett
Homer Gordon
Ruby Benford
Arma Gene Wiseman
Napolean Harrison
Eddie Mae Hackett
Pearl Bagsby
Willie Mae Tate
Otis Wheeler
Sam "S. C." Young, Jr.
Opalene Isaac
Cora Williams
Mable Cooper
The Bookers
Walter "Dago" Harris
Hood Taylor
The Atkinsons

Although an area of town established primarily for black citizens of Broken Bow, a few Choctaw Indian families resided in the Quarters on the west side near the Spray Pond. Noted Indian families residing in the Quarters included the Wilson, Shomore, Winship, and the Harris families. Relationships among the two races were very cordial.

Dierks Lumber Company provided the primary source of employment for Broken Bow residents during the early years. Employees were for the most part satisfied with wages and salaries they received during this time. In fact, most were happy to simply have a job. However, history records two disputes with the lumber company concerning wages.

In the 1940s organized labor and the Committee for

Industrial Organization (CIO) began organizing lumber industry employees. Dierks workers at Wright City, Clebit, and Broken Bow held a two-month long strike in 1947 and won an eight-cent per hour pay increase. Again in 1955, workers went on strike in mills and logging camps in Wright City, Broken Bow, Clebit and Blakely.

The 1955 strike created severe tension and strife among Dierks lumber workers, both blacks and whites. Some employees who were not union members refused to honor the strike and attempted to cross picket lines to continue working. These non-union members were labeled as "scabs". It has been speculated that the 1955 strike was not merely intended for an increase in wages, but also an attempt by the union to force the Dierks Lumber Company to require all employees to join and pay monthly dues.

Workers picketed Dierks for six months, enduring much hardship because of the lack of income during the strike. The strike was particularly difficult on black workers because most had no savings to fall back on. Ultimately, the employees returned to work, calling off the unsuccessful strike.

A welcome aide during the time of the strike was a program sponsored by the United States Department of Agriculture (USDA). This program distributed commodities to needy families and to Indian Reservations. The program was a blessing as food items such as cheese, rice, flour, powdered milk, butter, pork, and gravy sustained many black families. The program was administered in McCurtain County by the county commissioner. Once each month, families black and white would report to the County Barn to receive their rations.

EARLY RESIDENTS OF QUARTERS

Willie Lee Jordan, Sr. and Mildred Jordan later moved to New Addition.

Clarence "C. J." Pennington, Jr.

Marvin Kennybrew was married to Crossie Mae Amos.

Flossie Mae Carter, nee Amos, at the age of 21.

BLACK COMMUNITIES AND THEIR CITIZENS 39

Brothers Levolia Brewer and Jack Brewer.

Opalene Carter and Bertha Lewis.

Archie D. "Mr. Ted" Cole.

Earnestine Cherry, nee Jordan.

BLACK COMMUNITIES AND THEIR CITIZENS

K.C. Jones.

Clarence Pennington, Sr.

Taylor Elder and Catherine King.

Narvel Jordan and Earnestine Jordan.

Albert Jordan and President Carter, Sr.

Herman Dean Carter.

Flossie Mae Jordan Carter, age 28, at the time of her first marriage to Albert Jordan.

Sid Smith.

BLACK COMMUNITIES AND THEIR CITIZENS

Elzie Lee King.

Opalene Carter.

Crossie Mae Kennybrew, nee Amos.

Edgar Garrett, Mrs. Annie V's husband.

Chapter 5
CHURCHES

In most small rural black towns, churches played a vital role in the community. This was true of Broken Bow as well. Six churches served the black communities of Broken Bow. Early pastors of Macedonia, a Baptist church located at 105 Washington Street in New Addition, were A. W. Williams and M. T. Crawford. A Holiness Church, built by Mrs. Fannie and H. O. Williams using their own funds, is located north of Macedonia on Washington Street. These churches remain active today in the New Addition area.

St. John's Baptist was moved from the Quarters and is now located in the Pine Park area east of Broken Bow.

In Pleasant Valley, there were three churches. Bethlehem Baptist Church has a long list of pastors who served for short periods of time. Early pastors include Reverends J. S. Noble, C. L. Gafford, and E. D. Graves. Reverend Major on several occasions served as interim pastor at Bethlehem when the church was without a permanent pastor. Faithful members of Bethlehem Baptist included Jodie and Pinky Burris, Roy Kennybrew and Mrs. Neely, Mr. Zanders and Mrs. Roberta Burris, Roy and Johnny Kate Davis, Otis and Addie Carson, Edna Brown Duckett, and Lillie Bell Duckett. Louisa Davis and Maye Helen Leffall, nee Arnold, served as Sunday School teachers at Bethlehem.

Up the lane in Pleasant Valley there were two churches. Hills Chapel, a Methodist Church, was pastured by Reverend McKissic and a Presbyterian Church was pastured by Reverend Allen Meacham. Prominent members of the Methodist Church were Adell and Delcia Lewis, Lonnie and Mary Bell Cooper, Martin and Gertrude Lewis, and Mr. and Mrs. Bryant Lewis, among others.

Faithful members of Reverend Meacham's Presbyterian Church included W. L. and Pearl Richards and their children Erma, Ina Mae Christina "Feddie" Richards, and W. L., Jr., known as "Dub". Others include the Bizzells, Mrs. Johnnie Bell, Ollie Duckett, Sammy and Theresa Duckett, Isaac and Juliann Burris, and Mr. and Mrs. Calvin Burris.

These churches served the Pleasant Valley residents. Each church was small in membership but served as a vital source of inspiration to community members. Christmas services were rotated annually between the churches and members from all three churches would gather to celebrate the event. Traditional songs of Christmas such as "The First Noel", "Away in a Manger", "Oh Little Town of Bethlehem", and "Oh Come all Ye Faithful" always were sung.

There was always a big, beautifully-decorated Christmas tree with bags of fruit and hard candy under the tree for each of the youth. These Christmas bags would be passed out to the kids of each family at the conclusion of the Christmas program. Some youth, who were college students, received money as a form of scholarship to assist with their cost of continuing their education.

Generally the Christmas services concluded with the singing of "Silent Night." This was a special and very meaningful event, particularly, for the children because in some instances the fruit and candy might be the only Christmas treat they would receive.

During Christmas, it was common for adults to visit between neighboring homes on Christmas morning using the expression "Christmas give", a term long since forgotten in today's vernacular. The expression had no real significance but was simply a black form of greeting at Christmas time.

Vacation Bible School was another event that youth looked forward to each summer. The youth membership in each of these churches was rather small; consequently, this event also was shared between the church families in the summer. Regardless of which church hosted Vacation Bible School, the daily activities of singing, reading Bible stories, coloring, drawing pictures, and other art projects were similar. However, those hosted at Reverend and Mrs. Meacham's church seem the most memorable. Of the three churches located in Pleasant Valley, the Methodist Church, Hills Chapel, is the only one still active today.

Black gospel quartets were popular in the churches during this era. Most noted in Broken Bow was a group called the "Spiritual Five". Members included Ollie Duckett, Rastus "Bo Do" Burris, James "Pip" Burris, Ruby Carter, and Bertha Lena Burris. The group was manager by W. T. Holmes and performed regularly in the surrounding local churches.

Later, a similar group called the "Ebony Gospel Trumpets" was formed which included some of the original members of the Spiritual Five, but later expanded to include Ollie and Sammy Duckett, Dennis Hill, Larkin Wimbley, Charles and Carl Kennybrew, Homer Gordon, Rastus Burris, and James Burris.

In Idabel there was a gospel group called the "Mighty Clouds of Joy". Mrs. Hattie Valentine, a female gospel musician had a fifteen-minute radio program that was aired weekly over station KBEL in Idabel. Most black families faithfully tuned in to the program to hear Mrs. Valentine sing.

Chapter 6
ENTREPRENEURS & SUCCESSFUL DUNBAR GRADS

Entrepreneurship and business operations were unique in the town of Broken Bow during the early years. The lumber company paid its workers bi-monthly; however, for those who could not wait until payday they could go to the company's main office and secure coupons that could be used as legal tender for purchasing and paying bills in town. The coupons came in booklets ranging from 5 cents up to 20 dollars in denomination. Blacks relied heavily upon the coupons to get them from one pay period to the next. This practice became so prevalent that the main office of the lumber company became known in the black community as the "coup office".

As one would expect, most black adults were employed by Dierks and worked as laborers at the sawmill; however, some bootlegged and sold moonshine whiskey to make a living. The topography around Broken Bow made for a relatively safe and a perfect layout for moonshine whiskey stills. Corn, sugar cane, clean water, a heating stove, and copper tubing was all that was needed to fire up a productive liquor still.

Whites for the most part owned and operated the whiskey stills; however, many blacks sold the moonshine or "cat liquor" as it was called, to earn money. It was common for a moonshine still operator to make upwards of $400 to $600 dollars a week selling moonshine. This compares to the local county commissioner who made $50 per week. The average local worker made approximately $12 to $15 dollars per week as a laborer during this time. Obviously, operating whiskey stills was a more lucrative business.

Because whiskey stills were illegal, when or if a still operator was apprehended they would plead guilty to the charge, maybe be sentenced to a few months in jail, and most often released early for good behavior. The only real damage to the still operator for the most part was to his reputation in the community.

A number of blacks were entrepreneurs and ran their own businesses. Mr. V. L. Mills was the first proprietor of the boarding house in the Quarters. The boarding house was an establishment built and owned by the Dierks Lumber Company. Single men could rent rooms and eat daily meals at the boarding house. It had domino tables, pool tables, a jukebox, and dance floor. The boarding house served as a social gathering place for Quarters' residents. During later years, Curtis Cantley and Bee King operated the boarding house.

A memorable, yet unfortunate, incident occurred at the boarding house when it was alleged that Catherine King shot and killed her husband Cliff after a domestic argument.

The incident spurred a month long trial that was held at the county courthouse in Idabel. Interested black residents packed the courthouse chambers daily to hear testimonies and to witness the outcome of the trial. Because of inconclusive evidence and conflicting testimonies surrounding the incident, Mrs. King was acquitted and did not serve any time for the shooting.

Mr. Banks operated a small grocery store one block from the Dunbar School. At noon students regularly frequented the store and for around 25 cents could purchase three or four slices of bologna, crackers, and an orange soda. Sid Smith, K. C. Jones, A. D. Bennett, W. C. Butler, Simon Burris, and Clifford Carter were barbers. In addition to being a barber, W. C. Butler ran a small store out of his residence selling candy, bubble gum, cookies, and soda pop.

Annie V. Garrett operated a café in New Addition for several years that was a favorite spot for adults to spend their leisure time and money. Adell Lewis operated two different grocery stores in Pleasant Valley. Each store was destroyed by fire. Although never documented, it was suspected that another local grocery store owner might have been responsible because of the competition. Lewis made a final attempt to build a third store. However, it was never completed and the unfinished building still stands at the entrance of Pleasant Valley.

Arthel Burris operated two cafes, both called the Jolly Inn. Both also were destroyed by suspicious fires. Suspicion also surrounded these burnings because of the continual complaining by white citizens that asserted the cafes were too noisy and the loud music was a disturbance to the community.

Perhaps the most successful black entrepreneurs were ranchers. Sam Hill and his wife owned their home and a large section of land south of Broken Bow where he raised and sold livestock. Ivory Butler, Jodie Burris, Roosevelt "Pluck" Lewis, Clint Williams, and Jake Walker also were well-respected ranchers in the black community. It was common to see them riding tall on their beautiful ponies fully attired in boots, spurs, and chaps exhibiting the look of true cowboys and cattlemen.

Mrs. Willie Mae Cole operated a small barbecue business out of her home where she sold sandwiches, ice cream cones, and an assortment of other items. Reedy Macque Spigner, son of Professor Spigner, Dunbar's last principal, became a prominent attorney in Plano, Texas.

James Edward Carter and Ardis Cubit were 1958 graduates of Dunbar High School. Carter and his wife Frances managed more than fourteen franchises of Oscar's Restaurants, a subsidiary of Food Makers in San Diego, California, before his retirement. After a long and successful career with Demco, Cubit started his own heating and air conditioning business in Oklahoma City.

Winzel Lee Hamilton is a successful independent insurance agent with Jackson National Life Insurance Company, a subsidiary of Prudential Corporation in Portland, Oregon. Ike Maddock manages a large acreage of land in Longview, Texas where he raises cattle and grows hay.

Theodis Kennybrew, a 1958 graduate of Dunbar High School, began his career with the Los Angeles Unified School District while investing in real estate. After retiring, he continued to look for opportunities to invest in and owns numerous properties in the Los Angeles, California, area.

After retiring from the paper mill in Valliant, Dunbar High School 1960 graduate Vernell Ramsey also has become a prominent real estate entrepreneur in Broken Bow. Vernell owns several lots and homes in the New Addition and Pleasant Valley area.

Bryant Lewis' daughters have had successful professional careers. Christine Lewis Ratcliff is currently the director of grants and contracts for Rust College in Holly Springs, Mississippi; Bertie Mae Lewis retired after a successful teaching career; Mary Lou Lewis is retired after a successful accounting career for Sears; and Tomycine Lewis retired after an extensive tenure with the Oklahoma Blood Institute (OBI) in Oklahoma City.

After several years of teaching, Anna Faye Lewis completed her career as a psychometrist, testing students throughout the Kansas City school system. Ruth Lewis, a 1964 Dunbar graduate and salutatorian of her class, is a registered nurse and teaches at the Kiamichi Technical Center in Idabel. Gertrude Lewis had a storied career as a Dunbar/Broken Bow High faculty member.

Della Cooper Ivory, a 1964 Dunbar graduate, is retired after forty combined years of teaching elementary education in both the Kansas and Texas school systems. Ivory and her husband Donald currently reside in Missouri City, Texas. Maxcine Lewis Bostic, class of 1958, is noted as an outstanding and well respected educator, teaching for a number of years in Boswell and Wichita, Kansas before retiring. She currently resides in Okmulgee.

If not the most, certainly one of the most successful Dunbar graduates is Maye Helen Arnold Leffall. Born in Broken Bow and raised in the Pleasant Valley community, she graduated as the valedictorian of the 1958 Dunbar High School Class. After graduation, she relocated to Los Angeles, California, and attended Los Angeles City College before transferring and receiving her Bachelor of Arts degree in sociology/social welfare from California State University in 1963. She earned her Master's of Social Work from the University of Southern California in 1969 and a Master's in Biblical Counseling and a Doctor of Philosophy in Religious Studies summa cum laude from Long Beach Bible College in 2009. Maye Helen Leffall, MSW, LCSW, CCFC, M.B.C., Ph.D., is a licensed clinical social worker, clinically certified forensic counselor, clinical supervisor, consultant, and educator. During the majority of her career until her retirement, she worked as a children's services worker, supervisor, program analyst, child and family therapist; and field instructor for Los Angeles County and the graduate schools of social work at California State University, Long Beach (CSULB), University of California at Los Angeles (UCLA), and University of Southern California (USC).

Following retirement, she joined the faculty at USC as assistant clinical professor of social work, field education coordinator, and student advisor. Leffall is currently a professor at Long Beach Bible College where she teaches Christian Counseling and Christian Ethics courses. She is married to Dr. Reginald Mack Leffall, III, pastor of Tabernacle of Faith Baptist Church in Los Angeles where she is actively involved in the various ministries of the church. She and her husband live in Carson, California.

A modest individual, I have listed only a small portion of her accolades and accomplishments as her complete vita would encompass several pages. Leffall is a devout Christian, has traveled worldwide, including travel to the Holy Land, and credits all her accomplishments to her Lord and Savior Jesus Christ. *"Congratulations Maye Helen, you make all Dunbar graduates proud"*.

These are just a few of the Dunbar High School graduates and former Broken Bow residents who went on to achieve success in the business world. The list could go on and on but would be much too lengthy for one volume.

Runion "Champ" Hendricks also could be called an entrepreneur. He was known to be one of the best black shade tree mechanics in McCurtain County. He could fix any car regardless of the year, make, or model. He could pull an entire engine from a vehicle, perform a complete overhaul, and reinstall the engine and have the car purring like a kitten in a few days. The amazing part of all this is he used only basic tools—screwdrivers, wire pliers, ball ping hammers, and maybe a few socket wrenches. He had no diagnostic equipment and performed all repairs simply from experience or in some cases through trial and error. His charge for doing simple repair jobs such as changing belts, radiator hoses, u-joints, minor tune-ups, or brakes was minimal and in some cases the cost might merely be a pint of corn whiskey.

Runion always had been a law-abiding citizen. Yet, for reasons not clearly known, he once got himself into some minor trouble with the law and had to spend time in the Idabel jail. Runion was a large muscular man and while incarcerated he sustained some severe head injuries. The story was told that he had become unruly because he did not like being locked up. Police authorities reported that he had banged his head against the cell floor or cell bars which caused the injuries. Speculation was that he had been beaten by the jailers. I suppose the only ones who know what really happened would be the officers and Runion; however, he never divulged what actually took place. Those who visited Runion during the time he was incarcerated reported that he often sang or quoted the following lyrics while in jail;

Now let me tell you a little story
That some of you may not know
It's a hard time in the Idabel jail.

If you can't pay your bail
You have to stay in your cell,
It's a hard time in the Idabel jail.

Now, to all of you listen up good
Do what's right and the things you should
Cause it's a hard time in the Idabel jail
It's a hard time in the Idabel jail.

Now old Gene Harris, he thought he was tough,
Until he ran against Brother Joe Hough,

Cause it's a hard time in the Idabel jail.
It's a hard time in the Idabel jail.

  Though not necessarily true entrepreneurs, Curtis Cantley and Martin Lewis worked for Jewel Callaham as telephone engineers. Whenever something went wrong with the phone lines, Cantley or Lewis was immediately on the scene to repair the lines or phones. It was inspiring to many young black youth, including this author, to see these men strap on their spike boots and climb telephone poles to do their work. It gave many black youth encouragement to know that they too might one day have an opportunity to do something other than work as a laborer at the Broken Bow sawmill.

While on the subject of entrepreneurship and work, it would be an injustice if reference was not given to one of Broken Bow's citizens who is respected by the entire community. It is with great pleasure and tremendous pride that Willie Lee Jordan, Jr. is chronicled in this section.

Willie Lee Jordan, Jr.

A 1963 graduate of Dunbar High School, Jordan attended Eastern State College in Wilburton for two years. He also attended Langston University in Langston. He later returned to Broken Bow and began working at the Tyson chicken plant approximately four and ½ miles south of the city. Willie Lee Jordan, Jr. has worked at the plant for forty years without one single day of absence. His picture hangs on the wall in the plant in recognition of his diligence and perfect attendance.

The amazing part of this story is Jordan does not drive. He has had to secure a ride to and from the plant daily for his entire forty years. He says he is giving consideration to retirement at the end of this year. *"Hooray to Willie Lee Jordan."* If Willie does retire, the Tyson Plant should throw the biggest retirement ceremony in the company's history in recognition of Willie's loyalty and dedication to work and the company.

One might say Willie is a "chip off the old block". His father, Willie Lee Jordan, Sr. had a similar work record when he worked for Dierks Lumber Company and later Craig Fiber Plant east of Broken Bow. Willie Jordan, Sr. seldom missed work and often went to work even when he was sick. It has been said that one of his favorite sayings was "even a blind sow will find an acorn if she roots long enough".

Earnestine Cherry, the senior Jordan's sister, acquired the same work ethic. Cherry began working at the age of sixteen. She did "day work" for Rex Chandler for numerous years. Earnestine could be said to have been the "Nanny" for Harold Chandler, Rex Chandler, Jr., Paul Chandler, and Granville Chandler. Cherry and her husband Manuel later moved to San Diego, California, where she raised four children of her own. While in San Diego, she continued doing day work, this time for Mrs. Winn. She retired following Mrs. Winn's death.

John Jordan

John Jordan, one of the senior Jordan's sons, recently retired from Solar Turbine and Engines Corporation and resides in San Diego, California. Two other brothers, Michael Jordan and Bradley Jordan, live and work in Oklahoma City. Each has amassed similar work records as Willie Lee Jordan, Jr. Again, it is most appropriate and fitting to commend this family for their outstanding work ethic.

Chapter 7
THE SCHOOLS

Schools in Broken Bow were segregated until 1965. Two black schools existed prior to integrations. The first school established for blacks was a small one-room building south of Broken Bow in the Pleasant Valley community and Lucretia Richards was the first teacher.

Students Gertrude Lewis and Earnestine Jordan attended this early Pleasant Valley school. Lewis reported that her father, Adell Lewis, brought her to school each day on the back of a mule. Often on Fridays, Mrs. Richards had to leave school early and would leave Lewis in charge of the class. The school consisted of grades one through eight. The school known as Dunbar would come later.

The first facility known as Dunbar was built in the early 1920s. The school was located on the east side of New Addition. The principal was Professor Charles Hughes and Rixie Gates was the teacher.

Mr. Lewis now brought his daughter Gertrude to school, now located in town, in a cattle truck because of the longer distance to travel. Such commitment to securing an education was the impetus that spurred a lifelong love for education in his daughter's life and was the beginning of her long and distinguished career in teaching.

Later a remodeled building was erected for Dunbar students located in the same location east of Broken Bow. For the first time, this school was called "Dunbar High School" because it consisted of grades one through twelve.

The first principal of Dunbar High School was Professor Kennon. Reedy Mack Spigner became Dunbar's second principal. The school experienced its greatest expansion under the leadership of "Prof. Spigner" as he was affectionately called. In the mid-1950s under Professor Spigner's leadership the school was renovated and a gymnasium was constructed primarily using student labor. The new renovations consisted of the principal's office, seven classrooms, two bathrooms, a stage, and a gymnasium with two athletic dressing rooms. The gym had a high pitched arched roof with diamond shaped rafters in the ceiling which was the design of Professor Spigner.

Eventually Dunbar became part of the Broken Bow school system, governed by the local school board and Superintendent Rector Johnson. Black students were bused from Pleasant Valley, Lukfata, and Eagletown as agriculture, shop, and home economics classes were added to the Dunbar curriculum.

The school operated until 1965 at which time the schools in Broken Bow were integrated. The Dunbar buildings remained for a short time thereafter and operated as Eastside Junior High School until the school burned. The school was gone but the memories have never been forgotten.

YOU LAID THE FOUNDATION
"I thank my God upon every remembrance of you" Phil. 1:3

Separate but equal was the law that permitted segregation during this time. Although beloved by its students and the community, Dunbar High School was anything but equal. The curriculum was limited and the school never received equal funding per student as did the white school.

continued on page 66

PRINCIPALS AND TEACHERS O

Lucretia Richards
First Teacher in Pleasant Valley

Charles Hughes
First Principal in New Addition

Rixie Gates
First Teacher in New Addition

Professor Kennon
First Principal of Dunbar High School

R. M. Spigner
Second Principal, Math Teacher, and Football Coach of Dunbar High School

Geneva Spigner
Math and English Teacher

Catherine Spigner
English Teacher and Girls Basketball Coach

Rosella S. Barr
Home Economics Teacher

Gertrude Lewis
Elementary Teacher

Garfield Johnson
Coach and Vocational Agriculture Teacher

Jeanetta Johnson
Social Studies/Government Teacher

Fannie Williams
Science Teacher

Mary B. Cooper
Elementary Teacher

Hazel M. Alford
Elementary Teacher

George Shaver
Teacher and Band Director

Mrs. Hodge
Junior High Teacher

Mrs. B. Williams House
Elementary Teacher

Mrs. Harris
Elementary Teacher

Dunbar students are forever grateful to all Dunbar teachers.

DUNBAR

Jimmy Carter
Band Teacher

Violet Marrow Echols
Elementary Teacher

B. N. Brown
Assistant Coach and Band Teacher

L. D. Bennett, Jr.
Band Teacher

Herman Stewart
Band Teacher

Pearletta Gray
Typing Teacher

Edward House
Woodwork/Shop Teacher

Mrs. E. D. Anderson
English and Typing Teacher

Irma Anderson Shaver
Typing Teacher

A COLLAGE OF SOME DUNBAR TEACHERS

MORE TEACHER COLLAGES

Dunbar school colors were maroon and black; however, due to inadequate budgets Dunbar Band Students never owned uniforms and performed in parades and at halftime of footballs games in black and gold uniforms donated from the white high school.

continued on page 69

STUDENTS FROM EAGLETOWN

Black students from Eagletown became an integral part of Dunbar High School. A partial list of students from Eagletown who attended Dunbar are:

Gloria Parker
Magdaline Parker
Robbie Parker
Ike Polk
Leon Polk
Doris Polk
Floyd Wimbley
Larkin Wimbley
Virginia Wimbley
Charles Wimbley
Charlie Burris
Mae Anna Burris
Ray Burris
Daisy Johnson
Elsie Mae Warner
Helen Wimbley
LaVern Brown
Thelmarie Lewis
Maxcine Lewis
Clarence Lewis
Rueben Dale Lewis
Laura Ruth Lewis
Rosetta Lewis
Gary Grant Lewis
Parthenia Owens
Clyde Owens
Carl Lewis
Alice Faye Smith
Anna Kay Lewis
Helen Johnson
Ola Faye Stafford
Jessie Lee Owens
Ola Mae Johnson
Earnest Parker

The irony is, Eagletown was approximately 6 miles east of Broken Bow and funds were available to bus students from there, yet, early on, the school district supposedly could not afford the funds to provide a bus route that could pick up the black students in the Quarters. Obviously, the issue was not funding, but doing whatever was necessary to maintain segregation. If funding had truly been the primary issue and cost was the determining factor, why were black students bussed past white schools and white students bussed past black schools? Surely it would have been more cost effective to bus students to the school nearest their residence.

STUDENTS FROM THE QUARTERS

Initially, black students from the Quarters walked approximately 1½ miles through the "Pole Yard" to and from Dunbar daily as buses were not used to pick these students up at the time; however, later on, buses were permitted to include the Quarters' students in their routes. Not complete, but a list of the early students who made the trek each day were:

Evelyn Jo Cole
C.J. Pennington
Lonzo Broussard
Cleo Broussard
James E. Broussard
Kenneth Broussard
Vinnie Mae Broussard
Opal Broussard
Ivory Broussard
Katy Broussard
Mary Broussard
Cornell Burris
Ollie Bessie Miles
Olivia Jordan
Willie L. Jordan, Jr.
Dorothy Ann Burris
Edith Burris
Odell Hankins
Landon Hankins
Daisy Hankins
Mozell Hankins
Minnie J. King
Elzie Lee King
Willie Lee King
Ola Mae Warner
Elmarene Warner
Wilber Jefferson Warner
M. J. Warner
Emma Lee "Pig" Elder
Mary Lee Elder
Maybell Pennington
Willie L. Jordan, Sr.
Earnestine Jordan
Johnnie B. Carter
Opalene Carter
Herman Carter
Ruby L. Carter
James E. Carter
Scarlett Carter
Clifford Carter
Fezell Frazier
Willie B. Frazier
Juanita Frazier
Willie L. Frazier, Jr.
Othell Sykes
Eddie Sykes
Odell Sykes
Willie Lee Sykes
Walter Trotter
Val Gene Golston
Charlie Golston
Billie Golston
Cecil Duckett
Donna Faye Duckett
Ardis Cubit
J. W. Cubit
Bobby L. Savage
Willie Ciscero
Taylor Elder
A. Z. "Mose" Cunts
Credell Pennington
Dave Williams

continued from page 66

Textbooks were passed down to Dunbar when the white school received updated textbooks. The same was true of buses. When the white school got new buses, the older buses were passed on to Dunbar for use.

Being a product of a black segregated school, there is no doubt in my mind that Dunbar students were limited in what they were exposed to academically due to no fault of its teachers. Nevertheless, what the students lacked academically, the teachers made up for through caring, nurturing, and hanging in there with the students when they faced difficult times or when the going got tough.

I say Dunbar students were limited because the curriculum did not include courses like chemistry and there were no science labs. No foreign languages were taught. Molecular biology, physics, and astronomy were absent. These are classes that were commonplace in the white high school and one would surely have to take most, if not all, of the above mentioned classes if they went on to college. Black students were not exposed to such classes at Dunbar, yet Dunbar teachers gave everything they had to their students. Saying that Dunbar Students were limited in what they were exposed to is simply "telling it like it was".

In spite of these disparities, Dunbar students succeeded. Teachers at Dunbar emphasized that failure was not an option. They instilled a "can do" attitude in every student. Dunbar teachers subscribed to the philosophical view that was prevalent at that time among historically black schools which emphasized "Each One Teach One". If a student was fortunate enough to be exposed to a broader curriculum, what he or she learned was then passed on to their fellow classmates. Dunbar graduated its first senior class in 1937.

Members of the 1937 class were Leola Bizzell, Roxanna Workman, Clint Williams, Beatrice Burris, Elizabeth Bizzell, Nathaniel Spigner, and Cleve Mills. *continued on page 74*

DUNBAR TEACHER'S

PROFESSOR REEDY MACK SPIGNER
Professor Spigner probably was ahead of his time. In mathematics he taught students things like the Pythagorean Theorem which states the square of the hypotenuse is equal to the sum of the other two sides. He taught that there were ascending numbers far above billions and trillions. He stated that there were such things as septillions, octillions, nonillions, decillions, and duo decillions. He informed us that there are just as many of these numbers below zero as there are above zero. Professor Spigner had a reputation of sometimes "blowing smoke", however, much of what he told his students oftentimes came to pass. He told his students that there would be cars in the future that one would not need to shift, but you would simply push a button to drive the car.

GARFIELD JOHNSON
Our agriculture teacher, Mr. Garfield Johnson taught us to wire houses, castrate pigs and cows, how to identify the various species of grasses, and how to roof homes. He was

Each of Dunbar's teachers had what one might call a "specialty".

SPECIALITIES

the sponsor for the New Farmers of America (NFA). Initiation into the NFA organization included wearing one of your pant legs rolled up above the knee and carrying a brick around school for several weeks. During the final week of initiation, you were taken to the school workshop, blindfolded and put through a series of events that included eating worms, really soft wet noodles.

MRS. ROSELLA BARR
In home economics, Mrs. Barr taught many of the Dunbar girls how to use a sewing machine and how to read patterns to make dresses and aprons. Some of the girls later in life became accomplished seamstresses. She taught the girls how to bake wholesome meals and proper table etiquette. The Dunbar girls became members of an organization called New Homemakers of America (NHA).

The Dunbar School's NFA and NHA organizations were the counterpart to the Broken Bow white School organization known as Future Farmers of America (FFA).

MRS. CATHERINE SPIGNER
Then, there was Mrs. Spigner who in English taught her students the parts of speech. She taught her students the various tenses of words and how to diagram sentences on the blackboard and to identify nouns, pronouns, verbs, and adverbs in every sentence.

MRS. FANNIE WILLIAMS
Mrs. Fannie Williams taught students to memorize and recite how blood is traced through the circulatory system of the body. She had her students recite and trace paths that food travels through the digestive system after eating a meal. She was a very religious person and each of her students can probably remember her quoting Revelation 21:8—all liars shall have their part in the lake which shall burneth with fire—when a student did not behave as she felt they should.

MRS. JEANETTA JOHNSON
Mrs. Jeanetta Johnson taught Dunbar students government and the various departments of our system of

government. She taught her students the composition or make up of both Houses in the United States Congress. Her students had to learn the requirements for becoming a member of the House of Representatives, the Senate, and the President of the United States of America.

MRS. MARY B. COOPER

Of course everyone knew that Mrs. Cooper was known as the expert when it came to public speaking. Anytime a student had to make a speech or do any form of public speaking, Professor Spigner would advise them to go see Mrs. Cooper so she could coach them in proper enunciation, voice, and diction.

MRS. GERTRUDE LEWIS

Mrs. Gertrude Lewis was known as a second mother to all the students in her classes. A former student of Mrs. Lewis related this story: *The County Health Department would come to Dunbar High School yearly to immunize every student. Mrs. Lewis was his homeroom teacher and he was frightened to death to*

take the shots. On immunization day, she gently put her arms around him, held his hand, and personally walked him through the shot line to ensure he remained calm. What a comfort. Thanks Mrs. Lewis.

MRS. HAZEL ALFORD

Mrs. Hazel Alford was Dunbar's music guru and played the piano for all the assemblies and the graduation exercises. Unlike white students who at graduation marched to "Pomp and Circumstance," every Dunbar graduate will remember the feeling that arose in their hearts as Mrs. Alford would begin playing Felix Mendelssohn's "War March of the Priest" when they started their march into the auditorium on graduation night.

The school operated a coop, cafeteria, which served lunch each day at a cost of 25 cents. Mr. Garfield Johnson ensured that "grace" was sung prior to every meal. The song's lyrics were:

>Thou are great and thou art good
>And we thank thee for this food
>By thy hand we must all be feed
>Give us Lord our daily bread
>Amen

Not all students could afford the 25-cent meals; therefore, some students worked in the cafeteria as servers and others washed dishes to cover the cost of their meals. Permitting students to work ensured that all students, regardless of their ability to pay, could eat a warm Lunch. The meals were wholesome and included a vegetable, a meat, a salad or coleslaw, bread, milk, and a dessert.

Among the cooks who prepared meals in the coop over the years were Willie Mae Tate, Martha Reynolds, Alice Burris, Martha Gray, Flossie Carter, and Pearl Savage.

Dunbar was not only a caring and nurturing school; it incorporated spiritual values in all of its activities and events. During the first period of each class day, students were required to have a short devotional lead by the students themselves. Generally the school song or "God Bless America" was sung; the Pledge of Allegiance was recited to emphasize patriotism, and in some instances a prayer might be given. There were no conscientious objectors to reciting a prayer and never were there any complaints from parents regarding constitutionality of praying in the public school. On the contrary, most parents expected these things to be done in school.

At the end of each football game all students in attendance would rush the field, gather around the team, and sing the school song. Before the beginning of each basketball game Mr. Garfield Johnson, the coach, insisted that the entire team gather around him, clasp hands and chant; all for one, one for all, all for Dunbar, Dunbar for all.

Students from Eagletown who attended Dunbar High School were temporarily absent from school several days in April 1953 due to a tornado that hit the town on April 23. An article by Tim Taugher of the *Big Springs Daily Herald*, in Big Springs, Texas, reported the following:

> EAGLETOWN, Oklahoma, (AP) – *A small tornado ripped through the Negro section of Eagletown last night, killing one person and injuring 12. All the victims were of the same family. Clarence Lewis Senior, the father of 10, was killed. All of Lewis's children, his wife and his father were seriously injured. Four houses were totally demolished by the storm, which residents called a "small tornado." Six other smaller homes were slightly damaged.*

Gary Grant Lewis, one of the Lewis children, said he always has felt it was a miracle that his father was the only one killed. According to Gary, his mother was seven months pregnant with his baby brother at the time the tornado hit, destroying their home. His grandfather also was in the house, so all total, according to Gary, there were thirteen individuals in the home. "Most of us were just young babies" said Gary, "but through the grace of God we all made it."

His father was 43 and his mother 35 at the time of the disaster. Gary Grant commends his mom for doing an awesome and tremendous job raising the family alone. "She was the greatest of mothers to us," according to Gary Grant.

Later, Mrs. Lewis moved the entire family to Broken Bow. She went on to raise all ten of her children on her own. They all attended Dunbar High School and each went on to college and became successful citizens.

Each school year at Dunbar always culminated with an end-of-the-year picnic. The entire school—students, teachers, bus drivers, and even parents—traveled to Beavers Bend State Park for the celebration. Individual teachers were responsible for making sandwiches, potato salad, and drinks for their classes. At noon all classes would gather in the picnic area to eat as a group.

When speaking with Dunbar graduates, it becomes evident that most are saddened by the fact that the old school site is no longer recognizable. The buildings are all gone and there is no evidence that Dunbar ever existed. That is why this book is so important; the author feels it is imperative that Dunbar graduates, their children, and grandchildren know and become aware of their parents' history and why they speak with such reverence when talking about their school. It may also explain to the children why their parents get so excited when the Dunbar reunion comes around. Our school song was not just a bunch of lyrics. Dunbar truly was a place that we loved so dear; and its name will forever ring in revere—"It's Dunbar High School that we love, just one more step and there is heaven above."

In tribute to all Dunbar High School graduates and as a legacy to its memories the author penned this poem:

Though the buildings are gone, do not despair
For our fond memories will always be there
Visions of the old school have slowly passed
But our fond memories will forever last
So stand tall and lift your heads high
For what was produced in the buildings will never die.

The author of this book would like to remind Dunbar graduates that, yes, the buildings are all gone but the buildings were simply brick and mortar. The true essence of what took place at Dunbar High School rest not in the buildings, but with the people it produced: Ike and Elmer

Maddock; Eiljah, Ulysses, Van, and Willie Isaac Burris; Cleon Hill; Clarence Radford; Pearly Mae, Charles, Carl, Wilma Jean, Theodis, William, and Harold Kennybrew; Earnestine, and Willie Lee Jordan, Sr.; C.J., Johnnie B., Opalene, Herman, Ruby, James, Scarlett, President, Jr., Sidney, and Patricia Carter; Bobby Faye, Ardis, Joe David, and Joe Walter Cubit; Della, Marylyn, and Carlos Cooper; and Gertrude, L.D., L.C., Walter, Willie, Garland, Anna Fae, Adell, Jr., and Ruth Lewis. Other members of the Lewis family include Christine, Tomycine, Mary Lu, and Bertie Mae.

Others include the Johnson family; Mary Vernell; the Spigners; Reedy Macque; Cedell, Dennis, Bonnie Mae, Lola, Opalene, Ora, Mary, LeVell, Pearl Anna and Leon Hill; Vernell, I. D., and Allen Ramsey; Jackie, J. D., Wilbur D., Sylvester, Burnell, and Charles Garrett; Ollie, Sammy, Ruben, and Lillie Bell Duckett; Clennon, Benny J., and LeVester Sykes; the Hamiltons; the Atkinsons; and many others that could be named.

Among Dunbar graduates, there are doctors, lawyers, pastors, college administrators, teachers, counselors, bankers, ranchers, security consultants, medical researchers, business entrepreneurs, secretaries, police officers, private investigators, and the list goes on. Regardless of the accomplishments or professions Broken Bow students have entered, it is a fact that whatever achievements they have obtained in life can be attributed in great part to the foundation given to them at Dunbar High School; the dedicated and nurturing teachers of Dunbar gave their all to their students.

When thinking of Dunbar High School teachers, a poem entitled "Sermons We See" comes to mind. The poem is taken from the book *The Light of Faith* by Edgar A. Guest.

SERMONS WE SEE
I'd rather see a sermon than hear one any day,
I'd rather one should walk with me than merely show the way,
The eyes are better pupils and more willing than the ear;
Fine counsel is confusing, but examples are always clear;
And the best of all preachers are the men, who live their creeds,
For to see the good in action is what everybody needs;
I can soon learn how to do it if you'll let me see it done,
I can watch your hands in action, but your tongue too fast may run.
And the lectures you deliver may be very wise and true;
But I'd rather get my lesson by observing what you do.
For I may misunderstand you and the high advice you give,
But there's no misunderstanding how you act and how you live.

Imperfect as they were, Dunbar teachers were the sermons most developing black students saw and observed as they began their lives growing up in Broken Bow.

continued on page 95

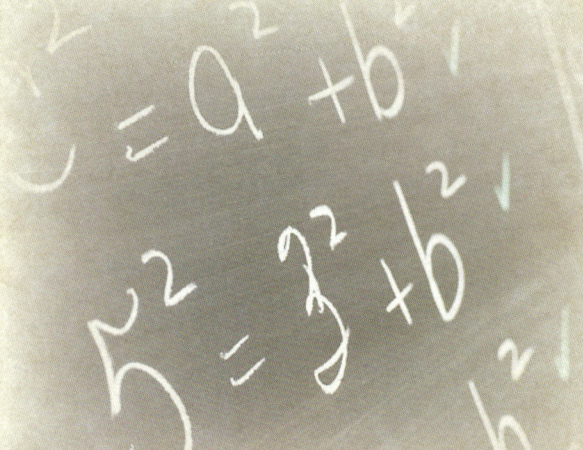

THE SCHOOLS

1952-1953 Senior Class

VARIOUS DUNBAR

Junior Class

TYRONE LYONS

CLARENCE RAMFORT

BYRD LEE LEWIS

CHRISTINE LEWIS

CAROLE HOLT

IRA MAE MARSHALL

BEVERLY JO SCOTT

ARTHELL DERBY

STACY WIDEMAN

Junior Class

CHARLES ROBERTSON

MILES ERA GARRETT

JUNE HAMILTON

IVORY LEE BUTLER

DOROTHY LEE NICKERSON

OLA MAE LEWIS

NAOVA LEWIS

J. D. GARRETT

JIMMY WALKER

1952-1953
Junior Class

CLASSES

1955-1956 Senior Class

Manuel Colbert
 (King)
    Charlyne Thomas
     (Stick horse)
        Jimmie Lee Lewis
         (Jim)

Alcleaita M. Atkinson
 (Tom)
    Lonnie G. Johnson
     (Lon)
        LeVester Sykes
         (Lee)

A. J. Laney
 (Laney)
    Florine Morris
     (Flo)
        Clenton Williams
         (Clent)

Lillie Bell Duckett
 (Lil)
    Lee Edward Alexander
     (Lee)
        Robert Richards
         (San Diego)

Verna Mae Burris
 (Fats)
    Robert Franklin
     (Little Frank)
        Essie Lee Jones
         (Essie Yok)

Clara Mae Walker
 (Clara, Winkty)
    Bobbie Fae Perry
     (Babe) (Bob cat)

THE SCHOOLS 83

1955-1956 Junior Class

1957-1958 Senior Class

THE SCHOOLS 85

Class of 1962

Bonnie Mae Hill, Bobby Faye Cubit, Maxine Bizzell, Rosetta Bizzell, Rodester Booker, and LeVester Sykes.

Mrs. Shaver's 1955 - 1956 Typing Class

1955-1956 Eighth Grade Class

Evelyn Cole
Charlie Golston
Charlie Wheeler
Vernell Ramsey

Mertha B. Butler
Ruthel Bizzel
William Kennybrew
Bertie Mae Lewis

Viney Broussard
Aurelia Parks
Arsenia Williams
Katie Mae Smith

Opaline Hill
J. W. Cubit
Gloria Gean Wheeler
President Carter Jr.

Minnie J. King
O. B. Burris
Carol Tate

JR HIGH SCHOOL 8TH GRADE CLASS OF 1956

1955-1956 Sixth Grade Class

I. D. Ramsey
Bobbie Munn
Adell Lewis

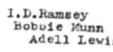   

Bernice Hackett
Norma Jean Issac
Kenneth Stuart

Herbert Lewis
Rosa Mae Walker
L. W. Lewis

Donnell Williams
Mary Florence Stuart
James Smith

Eather Lewis

THE SCHOOLS

FIRST ROW: *Paul Richards, Dorothy Ann Burris, Lola Hill, and Peggy Barr.*
SECOND ROW: *Sidney D. Carter, Willie Frazier, Jr., Mr. George Shaver, M.J. Warner, and Ora Lee Hill.*

Popular Characters

They Got Talent

1952-1953
Junior High Cheerleaders

LEFT TO RIGHT: Bonnie Mae Hill, Alcleata M. Atkinson, Anna Faye Lewis, and Scarlett O. Carter.

BELOW: Alcleata Atkinson, Scarlett Carter, and Rodester Booker.

BELOW: Dixie Jo Lewis, Maureen Richards, and Rosa Mae Walker.

ABOVE: Bonnie Mae Hill and Maxine Bizzell.

1952-1953 Midget Major and Majorettes

Mary Johnson, Charles Lewis, Rowena Atkinson, and Laureen Alford.

NHA girls modeling garments they made: LEFT TO RIGHT: Bonnie Mae Hill, Willie M. Bizzell, Scarlett Carter, and Dixie Jo Lewis.

NHA Girls in Action

NHA girls preparing fruit baskets for the shut ins of the community: Dorothy Butler, Mary L. Lewis, Alcleata Atkinson, Florene Morris, Mrs. Barr, Rodester Booker, Rosetta Bizzell, and Lillie Duckett.

Sophomore Football Queen 1948-1950

Ada Bell Cubit.

Homecoming Queen of Dunbar High School 1956

Miss Alcleata Marie Atkinson.

Miss Dunbar

Bertie Mae Lewis.

Football Team Homecoming Court 1961-1962

Mary Johnson, Laureen Alford, and Della Cooper.

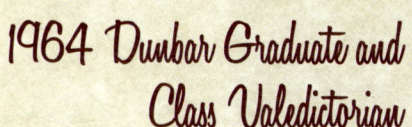

Reedy Macque Spigner, Tomycine Lewis, Charlyne Thomas Wysinger, and unknown.

1964 Dunbar Graduate and Class Valedictorian

Miss Laura Ruth Lewis.

1964 Dunbar Graduate

*Mrs. Della Cooper Ivory,
Alpha Sweetheart at Langston University.*

Best Friends
1964 Dunbar Graduates

Della Cooper Ivory.

Patricia Carter Hearne.

Dunbar High School as it existed prior to integration

The 1955 Panthers yearbook was dedicated to the completion of the new school and progress in education. The yearbook noted that the progress had been planned and directed by a foresighted administration and community leaders who were looking toward the future.

The yearbook noted that wise changes had occurred only as the planners were certain that the new building would bring great improvement over the old, and that the final result would be a school plant of which Dunbar students and faculty can feel justifiably proud. Administrators wrote the following upon completion:

We dedicate our yearbook therefore, to these already dedicated citizens of Broken Bow, who have made our school building, and school itself, possible for us.

Superintendent Rector Johnson
The Broken Bow School Board
Mr. Leon Lacy and Veteran Trainees
Mr. Edward House and Industrial Art Classes
Broken Bow High School
Dunbar Faculty
Patrons & Friends
Dunbar Student Body

BUS DRIVERS FOR DUNBAR HIGH SCHOOL

S. P. Hall	O. D. Brown	James Carter
Archie Earnest	Frank Burris	William Kennybrew
Bryant Lewis	Ike Polk	Sidney Carter
Sam Young	Martin Lewis	Paul Richards
Roy Davis	Ike Maddock	Jyles Walker
Willie Lee Reynolds	Eddie Sykes	Dennis Hill
	Herman Carter	

All the above were safe and accomplished drivers. Each was required to have a chauffeur's license in order to drive the bus. Sidney Carter and Paul Richards were only seventeen years old the summer before they were selected to drive the bus for Dunbar High School. Both had to attend a week long driver's training school in El Reno to obtain their chauffeur's license. Drivers had to be responsible and dedicated due to the fact that routes were quite long; consequently drivers had to begin early each morning to ensure students were at school on time.

Students were disciplined and seldom was there any trouble or misbehavior on the part of those who rode the bus.

Although all the drivers had excellent driving records, three bus drivers did have unfortunate incidents occur during their driving tenure.

While driving the Lukfata route, Willie Lee Reynolds encountered a drunk driver who had crossed the center line and was driving on the wrong side of the road. The result was a head-on collision that killed Jimmy Dowell. Fortunately, except for minor scratches and bruises, none of the students on the bus were severely injured.

Herman Carter drove the Pleasant Valley route which included picking up students from across the creek. Ruth Lewis wanted to get off the bus, an unscheduled stop, to go to her sister's house. Carter permitted the students to get off the bus up the lane from the Lewis home. Evidently, Mrs. Lewis was not at home; therefore, Ruth decided to walk back across the creek to her parent's home. Upon crossing the creek at the low water bridge, Ruth somehow fell into the water and nearly drown. Clarence Billie, a white citizen living nearby with his family, heard her cries and pulled her out of the Creek.

Herman felt responsible and never really got over the incident. Because Ruth was so young, he realized that he should have never allowed her to get off the bus alone. Afterwards, Herman stated many times he knew that Mr. Adell, Sr. and Mrs. Delcia would have never been able to forgive him for his poor judgment had Ruth drowned.

Mr. O. D. Brown, the Ealgetown bus driver, accidently backed over the infant child of Ola Mae and Rastus Burris when the child happened to get behind the bus, completely out of sight. Sadly the child was killed.

Other than an occasional breakdown, where a second bus had to be summoned to pick up students to get them home, no other notable bus driving incidents occurred.

HIGH SCHOOL COURTSHIPS

As is probably true of most high schools, Dunbar had its share of high school courtships. Most did not culminate in marriage, but a few did. A partial list of those "that did" result in marriage includes:

Aaron Carter and James Ell Elder
James Burris and Mary Elder
Clarence Pennington and Mozell Hankins
Rastus Burris and Ola Mae Warner

Manuel Cherry and Earnestine Jordan
Willie Lee Reynolds and Caroline Fulsom
Arthel Burris and Pearl Walker
Martin Lewis and Gertrude Lewis
Lonnie Cooper and Mary Bell Butler
Johnnie Carter and Dorothy Mae Burris
Willie Jordan and Mildred Pickens
Sam Young and Lilly May Hill
Val Gene Golston and Maxcine Bizzell
James E. Broussard and Lillie Bell Duckett
Eddie Sykes and Thelmarie Lewis
Clarence Lewis and Rowena Atkinson

A partial list of many other Dunbar High School courtships and romances "that did not" end in marriage includes:
Charles Kennybrew and Gloria Parker
Elijah Burris and Rosena Colbert
Jimmy Lee Love and Ruby Carter
Herman Carter and Louisa Mae Davis
Ardis Cubit and Olivia Jordan
LeVester Sykes and Bonnie Mae Hill
President Carter and Ruthel Bizzell
Charlie Golston and Robbie Parker
Vernell Ramsey and Bertha Mae Lewis
James Carter and Maye Helen Arnold
Willie Isaac Burris and Scarlett Carter
Thomas Colbert and Anna Faye Lewis
Sidney Carter and Della Cooper
Ruth Lewis and Reedy Macque Spigner
William Kennybrew and Opalene Hill
Bernice Hackett and Mary Hill
Charles Payne and Mary Vernell
Clarence Lewis and Patricia Carter

Paul Richards and Rosetta Lewis
John Jordan and Laureen Alford
Martin Warner and Maryann Colbert

DUNBAR PROMS

As with most schools, proms were a special event at Dunbar High School. Beginning in the early days, Dunbar sponsored a junior/senior prom each year. The proms generally had a theme of some sort. Junior and senior students would spend the entire week decorating the gymnasium for the prom.

For the boys, getting a date for the prom was usually a challenge because most of the boys had girlfriends who were under classmates, freshmen or sophomores. As a result, many went to the prom dateless.

For the girls, the prom dress was always a major concern. Many girls did not attend because they did not have what they deemed an appropriate prom dress.

It seems that with each prom some memorable event occurred that the participants always will remember.

For the 1955–1956 prom, Ruby Carter reported that for some odd reason her prom dress was not secured in time. Consequently, Janie Woods, a white student, loaned Ruby her prom dress. Janie was the daughter of Charlie Woods who owned a grocery store in Broken Bow.

Ardis Cubit reported that his date at the 1957-1958 prom was Olivia Jordan. Ardis stated he was dressed in a pristine white sport coat. The evening of the prom had torrential rain falling. Ardis recalls that as he was making his way to enter the gymnasium for the prom, he somehow slipped and fell into a puddle of water totally soiling his beautiful white sport coat.

He had to return home and change into a regular jacket before returning to the prom.

Manuel Colbert accidentally stepped on the hem of the dress of someone else's date and almost pulled the dress off the girl. We can laugh about these incidents now, but they were pretty embarrassing at the time.

The 1958–1959 prom of Anna Faye Lewis, Scarlett Carter, Bonnie Mae Hill, Val Gene Golston, Maureen Richards, and others centered around a theme called "The Sputnik", so named after the Russian spacecraft that was the first to orbit the Earth in 1957.

The 1962 prom was a combined event between Dunbar and Riverside high schools. The theme for the 1962 Prom was "An Evening in Paris". The gymnasium was decorated with red, white, and blue streamers and in the middle of the gym was a paper mache' image of the Eiffel Tower. Most memorable for the 1962 prom was the fact that three Dunbar girls did not return home immediately after the event. Names are intentionally withheld so as not to embarrass these girls. The morning after the prom, parents of these three girls were deeply concerned as to the girls' whereabouts. As it turned out, the three girls had taken a joy ride with some fellows after the prom and ended up in Powderly, Texas. The girls arrived home safely around 10:30 a. m. the next morning. Principal Spigner, teachers, and parents were extremely relieved when the girls made it back home without anything serious having happened.

DUNBAR REUNIONS

Currently, Dunbar graduates bi-annually host a reunion at the Broken Bow Eastside Community Center, the site where the school once stood. The reunion is held not only for old friends to reconvene, but also in an attempt to preserve the memories and traditions of the School.

Past reunion committee organizers have included: Mrs. Gertrude Lewis, Prema Lee Barr, Ruth Lewis McPowell, Mary Vernell Johnson Jackson, and Eloise Duckett. Other committee members who have assisted in the reunion planning include, Vernell Ramsey, Charles Kennybrew, Ray Burris, Willie Jordan, Jr., Sidney Carter, James Washington, Cecil Richards, Mary Hill Hawkins, Pearl Hill Hunter, and Bobby Morgan, among others.

There have been four reunions to date. The first reunion was held in 2003 followed by the 2005, 2007, and 2009 reunions.

Past keynote speakers for the reunions have been Maxcine Lewis Bostic (2003), Parthenia Owens Dillahunty (2005), Sidney Carter (2007), and Reedy Macque Spigner (2009).

The reunions originally started as a combined effort between Dunbar and Riverside high schools with graduates from both high schools participating. For reasons unknown, the Riverside group eventually pulled out of the event and the reunion is now strictly a Dunbar High School affair. Whatever the reason, the author feels it a great loss to not have Bill, James, and Cliff Cottons, Eloise Nelson Duckett, Ora Simmons, Lewis Austin, Paula Pillars Cotton, Bobby Morgan, Curtis Thompson, and other Riverside graduates as part of the reunion.

LeVell Hill, a security consultant, and his wife who now reside in Lucas, Texas, developed an outstanding website that graduates can access to stay informed as to what is being planned from year to year. The site also enables graduates to share their ideas for future reunions and view pictures of past reunions. All Dunbar graduates are encouraged to visit the site. The website is www.dunbarpanthers.com. *"Thanks LeVell".*

First Dunbar/Riverside Reunion - 2003

DUNBAR/RIVERSIDE
MINI REUNION
July 3rd - 6th 2003
AGENDA

July 3rd……………………………………………………….Registration

July 3rd...……………………….7:00 P.M…………..…………….Fish Fry

July 4th………………..……...6:00 P.M. ………..……………Banquet
   Keynote Speaker, Ms. Maxcine Lewis Bostic

July 4th…………………..………...7:30 P.M. ……..…… …Recognition Hour

July 5th ………………………12:00 noon…………………………Picnic

July 5th ………………………. 8:00 P. M…………………………. Dance

July 6th ………………….....................………..To To Church Somewhere!

Have a Safe Trip Home

Sidney Carter, Daisy Lewis Johnson, and Bernice Hackett.

RECOGNITION HOUR HELD AT GRAY HIGH SCHOOL IN IDABEL

Bernice Hackett, Alice Faye Smith Warner, Daisy Lewis Johnson, and Sidney Carter.

Second Dunbar/Riverside Reunion – 2005

Shelby Wilson, William Kennybrew, and Charles Henry Butler.

DUNBAR / RIVERSIDE REUNION 2005
SCHEDULE OF EVENTS

June 30, 2005

Register / Pick up Packets .... 10:00 – 3:00 pm
(Eastside Community Building – Dunbar School Site)
Fish Fry .... 6:00 pm
(Eastside Community Building – Broken Bow)

July 1, 2005

Social Hour .... Fun and Games .... 10:00 am – Until
(Eastside Community Building – Broken Bow)
Banquet, Keynote Speaker, Ms. Parthenia Owens Dillahunty .... 6:00 pm
Recognition Hour .... 7:00 pm
(Broken Bow Middle School – Broken Bow)

July 2, 2005

Picnic .... 1:30 pm
(Eastside Community Building – Broken Bow)
Alumni Meeting .... Let's Come together .... 3:00 pm
Dance / Social .... 8:00 pm
(Eastside Community Building – Broken Bow)

July 3, 2005

Let's Have Church .... 6:00 pm
(Macedonia Baptist Church – Broken Bow)

July 4, 2005

Open ....

Ardis Cubit and Ike Maddock.

J'Rae Lewis, Mrs. Gertrude Lewis, and Martin "M. J." Warner.

Clark G. Warren, Sidney Carter, and President Carter, Jr.

THE SCHOOLS

Reunion - 2005

Reverend Charles Kennybrew and Edward Jackson.

James Edward Carter, Clark G. Warren, Sidney Carter, and President Carter, Jr.

M. J. Warner, Jessie Mae Warren Ramsey, and Clark G. Warren.

Mrs. Gertrude Lewis, M. J. Warner, Reverend Charles Kennybrew, Edward Jackson, Theodis Kennybrew, and Isaiah Lewis.

J'Rae Lewis.

Third Dunbar/Riverside Reunion - 2007

Riverside Alumni

THE SCHOOLS

DUNBAR/RIVERSIDE REUNION
Keynote Speaker Sidney Carter
Banquet / Recognition Hour
July 6, 2007 • 6:30 P.M.
Idabel High School Cafeteria

Mary Jackson, Curtis Thompson, and LeVell Hill – M. C.'s

Order of Service

Call to Order .... M. C.

Song .... God Bless America

Prayer/Blessing of the Food

-Buffet-

Music

Welcome .... Eloise Duckett

Music

The Occassion .... Joyce McGuatha, and Vernell Ramsey

Recognition of Basketball / Football Teams .... Captains, or Players

Music .... Bobby Morgan

Introduction of Speaker .... A Carter Sibling (Mark Carter)

Keynote Speaker .... Sidney Carter

Entertainment .... Herman Stewart

Recognition of Teachers

Roll Call of Graduating Classes .... Dunbar / Riverside

School Song .... "   "

Memorable Memories

Closing Prayer

Back to Dunbar Center for the Dance

Johnnie Henderson and wife Scarlett Henderson.

Maxcine Lewis Bostic and Mrs. Elesta Williams.

Bernice Hackett and Patricia Carter Hearne.

THE SCHOOLS 109

President Carter, Jr. and Johnnie Mae Carter Burrell.

Daisy Lewis Johnson, Pearl Anna Hill Hunter, and Willie Frazier.

Mrs. Corine Pettis and Lillie Bell Duckett Broussard.

Reunion - 2007

Ike Maddock, Ardis Cubit, and Patricia Carter Hearne.

Charles Henry Butler and wife Jeannie.

Sidney Carter and son Mark Allan Carter.

Reunion - 2007

Ardis Cubit and wife Brenda Cubit.

Christine Kennybrew and President Carter, Jr.

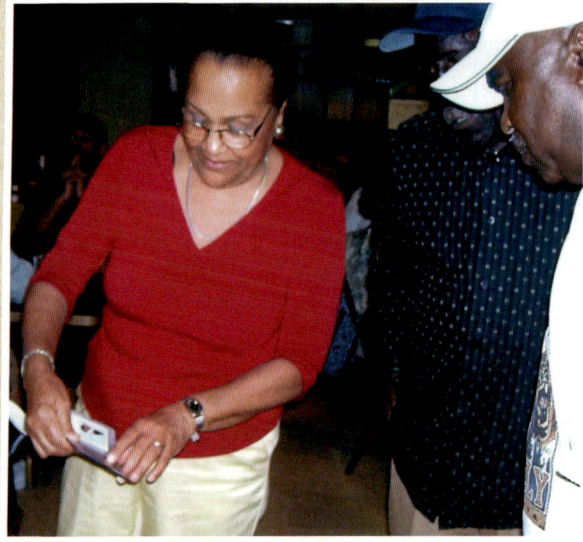

Scarlett Henderson, Walter Trotter, and Theodis Kennybrew.

BROKEN BOW'S BLACK COMMUNITIES AND DUNBAR HIGH SCHOOL

ABOVE: Corine Pettis, Clark G. Warren, Ardis and Brenda Cubit, and Cecil Richards.

Johnnie Henderson and wife Scarlett Henderson.

Maye Helen Arnold Leffall, Mark Allan Carter, and Sidney Carter preparing for the keynote address.

Reunion – 2007

Patricia Carter Hearne, Johnnie Henderson, and wife Scarlett Henderson.

Julius Lewis and Theodis Kennybrew.

Isaiah Lewis, Sidney Carter, and son Mark Allan Carter.

ABOVE: Cleo Bruossard, Walter Trotter, and Ike Maddock.

LEFT: Mrs. Johnnie Mae Carter Burrell.

Mrs. Corine Pettis, Patricia Carter Hearne, and President Carter, Jr.

THE SCHOOLS 115

President Carter, Jr.

Maxcine Lewis Bostic, Ike Maddock, Willie Frazier, and Charles Henry Butler.

Patricia Carter Hearne.

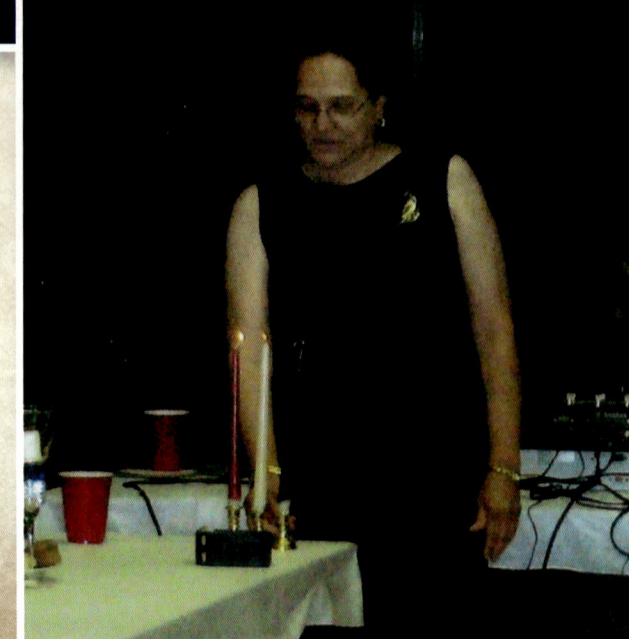

Reunion - 2007

Program MCs Mary Vernell Johnson Jackson and LeVell Hill.

Theodis and his wife Gloria Kennybrew, Christine Kennybrew, and President Carter, Jr. in the background.

Reunion – 2007

Theodis Kennybrew and Isaiah Lewis.

Reverend Charles Kennybrew, Johnnie Henderson, his wife Scarlett Henderson, and LeVell Hill.

BELOW: Claretha Butler Cubit, Charles Henry Butler and wife Jeannie. Reverend Charles Kennybrew is in the background.

Mrs. Corine Pettis and Lillie Bell Duckett Broussard.

Sidney Carter, Johnnie Mae Carter Burrell, and Willie Frazier. Consuelo Trotter is in the background.

Reverend Charles Kennybrew and Vernell Ramsey. Eloise Nelson Duckett is in the background.

Alice Faye Smith Warner and Ola Faye Stafford.

Pearl Anna Hill Hunter.

Eloise Nelson Duckett and Claretha Butler Cubit.

Reunion – 2007

Florene Morris and Ruby Jewel Green.

Maxcine Lewis Bostic.

Charles Henry Butler, Ardis Cubit and wife Brenda Cubit, Patricia Carter Hearne, Cecil Richards, and Johnnie Henderson.

Reunion – 2007

Donald Burris and his girlfriend.

Curtis Thompson and Mary Vernell Johnson Jackson.

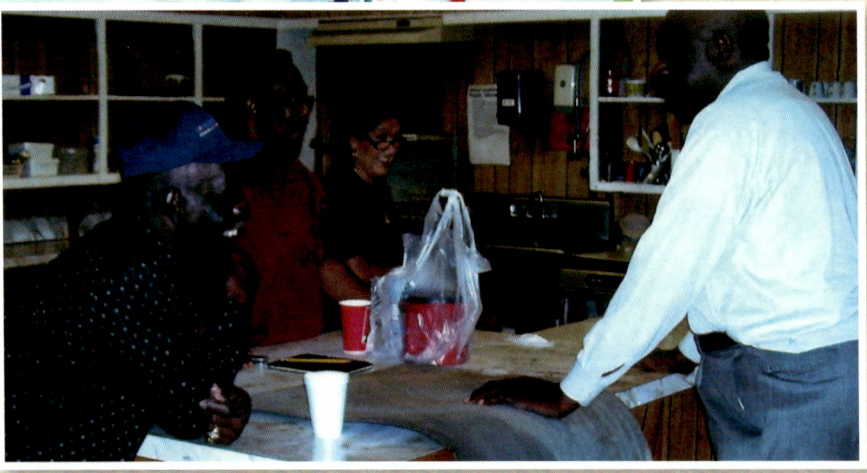

Walter Trotter, Willie Frazier, Consuelo Trotter, and Cleo Broussard.

Three Sisters—
Opalene Hill Cotton, Mary Hill Hawkins, and Pearl Anna Hill Hunter.

Reverend Charles Kennybrew and wife Christine Kennybrew.

Gloria Kennybrew, Florene Morris, Ruby Jewel, Theodis Kennybrew, Consuelo Trotter, and Walter Trotter.

THE SCHOOLS

Claretha Butler Cubit, Mrs. Corine Pettis, and Garnetta Johnson Sweet.

Mrs. Corine Pettis, Garnetta Johnson Sweet, and Opalene Hill Cotton.

Sidney Carter, giving the keynote address at the 2007 Reunion.

Reunion – 2007

Walter Trotter and wife Consuelo Trotter.

Pearl Ann Hill Hunter.

Reunion Planning Committee Vernell Ramsey, Sidney Carter, Mark Carter, Eloise Nelson Duckett, Reverend Kennybrew, and Bobby Morgan.

Joyce Nelson, Donald Burris, and girlfriend.

Sidney Carter and LeVell Hill.

Theodis Kennybrew and Walter Trotter.

Reunion - 2007

Cecil Richards.

ABOVE: Mark Carter, Sidney Carter, LeVell Hill, and Joyce Nelson.

Ruby Jewel, Florene Morris, and Isaiah Lewis.

THE SCHOOLS

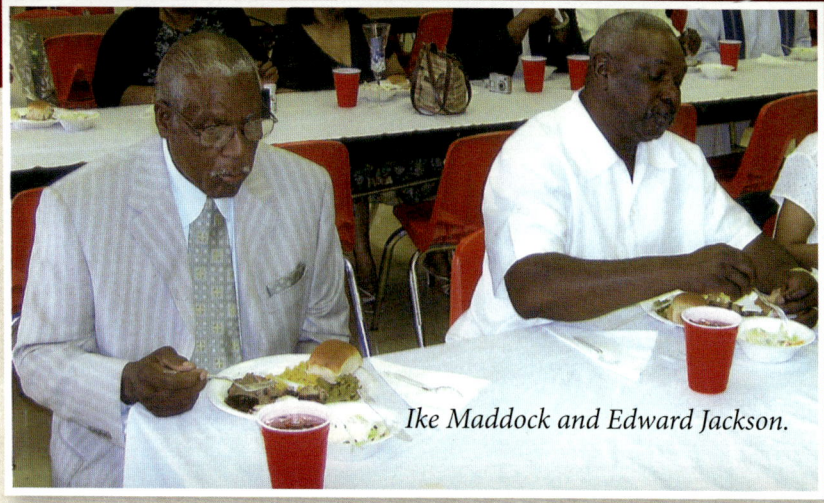

Ike Maddock and Edward Jackson.

Ola Faye Stafford, Alice Faye Smith Warner, and Loren Duckett.

Maxcine Lewis Bostic, her daughter, and Loren Duckett.

Reunion - 2007

Daisy Lewis Johnson and friend.

Cecil Richards and Charles Henry Butler with Linda Faye Smith and Johnnie Mae Burrell in the background.

Ike Maddock and LeVell Hill.

THE SCHOOLS

Reunion - 2007

Clark G. Warren, Mark Carter, and his dad Sidney Carter.

Della Eloise Cooper Ivory and LeVell Hill.

Harold Kennybrew and Opalene Hill Cotton.

130   BROKEN BOW'S BLACK COMMUNITIES AND DUNBAR HIGH SCHOOL

Isaiah Lewis, William Kennybrew, Mark Carter, and Sidney Carter.

LEFT: Wilber Jefferson Warner.

Mary Hill Hawkins.

Theodis Kennybrew and Ike Maddock.

Fourth Dunbar/Riverside Reunion - 2009

Keynote speaker for the 2009 Reunion Reedy Macque Spigner signing in with Edward Jackson in the background.

LeVell Hill and Cornell Burris.

Vernell Ramsey, Gloria Kennybrew, and Theodis Kennybrew.

Reedy Macque Spigner giving the keynote address at the 2009 Reunion; others pictured are Reverend Charles Kennybrew and his wife Christine, and Eloise Duckett.

BELOW: Reverend Charles Kennybrew and his wife Christine, Reedy Macque Spigner, and Eloise Duckett.

Reedy Macque Spigner and Garnetta Johnson Sweet.

Reunion – 2009

Ivory Lee Butler and Mary Vernell Johnson Jackson.

Reverend Charles Kennybrew, LeVell Hill, Reedy Macque Spigner, and Eloise Duckett.

Wilber Jefferson "Sonny" Warner.

ABOVE: *Reedy Macque Spigner, Sidney Carter, and Ike Maddock.*

Mary Vernell and Ike Maddock.

Vernell Ramsey and William Kennybrew.

Sidney Carter, Ike Maddock, and Charlyne Thomas Wysinger.

Reedy Macque Spigner, William Kennybrew, and Mary Vernell Johnson Jackson.

William Kennybrew in background, Walter Trotter, Consuelo Trotter, and Mrs. Corine Pettis.

Reunion - 2009

Mary Vernell Johnson Jackson and Reedy Macque Spigner.

BELOW: Walter Trotter and Ivory Lee Butler.

Reverend Bernice Hackett and his wife Sherlean, Christine Kennybrew and her husband Reverend Charles Kennybrew.

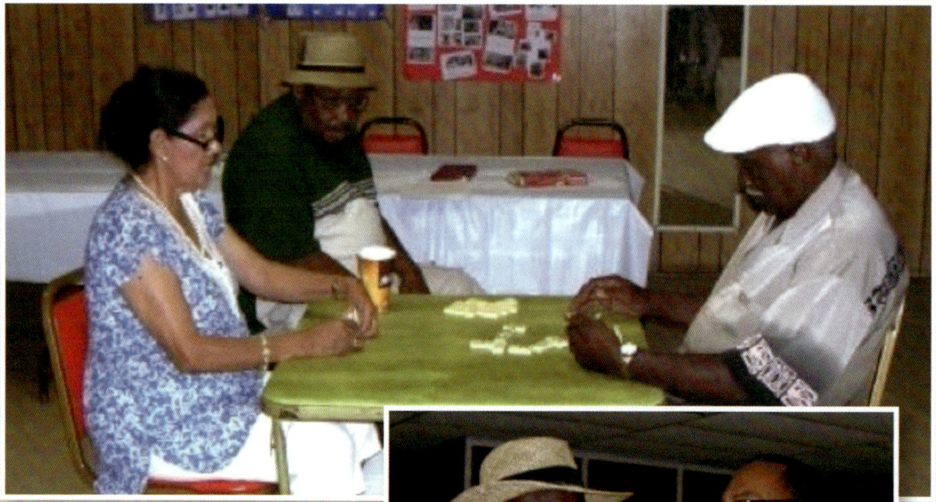

Reunion - 2009

ABOVE: Consuelo Trotter, wife of Walter Trotter, Wilber Jefferson Warner, and Vernell Ramsey.

Edward Jackson, Mary Vernell's husband, and Reedy Macque Spigner.

Sherlean Hackett, Christine Kennybrew, and Reverend Charles Kennybrew.

Sidney Carter.

Eloise Nelson Duckett, LeVell Hill, and Edward Jackson.

Claude Lee Cubit and wife Betty Cubit.

THE SCHOOLS 139

Chapter 8
SPORTS

The Dunbar High School Panthers have a rich and storied athletic history. Many outstanding athletes performed brilliantly for Dunbar. Unfortunately, none of these athletes ever received "All State" awards and most passed through Dunbar almost in utter obscurity except to the black community. This could be attributed in part due to the fact that their games were seldom, if ever, covered by sports reporters or newspaper articles outside of McCurtain County. Individual statistics and box scores went undocumented except in the school's personal scorebooks which have long since been lost or appear to be unrecoverable.

Due to segregation, in athletics, Dunbar was relegated to playing many Texas and Arkansas black schools. Obviously, not all the teams listed below were played in a single year; however, a typical schedule over the years would include teams from the following cities/towns.

ARKANSAS SCHOOLS
Minerals Springs   Washington
Ashdown   Foreman
Locksburg   Sitoka
Hope

LOUISIANNA SCHOOL
Bernice

FIRST ROW: G. B. Burris, Cleon Hill, Charles Burris.
SECOND ROW: Ruby Duckett, Floyd Wimbley, Jimmie Lee Love, Elmer Maddox.
THIRD ROW: Clarence Radford, J. D. Garrett, Herman Carter.
NOT SHOWN: Andrew Colbert, Eddie Sykes, Marvins Kenneybrew.
COACH: Mr. Garfield Johnson.

TEXAS SCHOOLS
Naples   Bonham   Honey Grove
Paris   Dangerfield   Cooper
Powderly

OKLAHOMA SCHOOLS
Frederick   Atoka   Colbert
Stillwater   McAlester   Sapulpa
Okmulgee   Idabel   Watonga
Hugo   Riverside (Harris) Wagoner
Boswell   Beggs

DUNBAR BASKETBALL TEAM

FIRST ROW: ROBERT RICHARDS, JAMES CARTER, MANUEL COLBERT, TERRY FRANKLING, ROBERT FRANKLINE
SECOND ROW: WALTER TROTTER, THOMAS COLBERT, ELBERT PAYNE, CLINTON WILLIAMS, EDWARD BURRIS
THIRD ROW: LORSE BEAL, CURTIS EARNEST, CHARLES BURRIS AND JOE DAVIS CUBIT.

COACH: GARFIELD JOHNSON

Panther Basketball

Dunbar had many good basketball teams. Dunbar played mostly black schools; however, when participating in the District Tournament at the end of the season, Dunbar did occasionally play white basketball teams. In fact, Dunbar played the Broken Bow Savages in basketball in the district tournament at Wright City during the 1957-1958 school year. During that year, the Broken Bow Savages had such standouts as Ray Hall, Ray Hicks, Jerry Dean, and Spotwood. Sadly, the Savages prevailed.

Other white teams the Panthers competed against in district tournaments were Rattan, Eagletown, Valliant, and Colgate.

The Dunbar basketball team played Eagletown in district play in 1960. Dunbar was without its leading scorer; President Carter, Jr. He was recovering from a deep thigh bruise and only played sparingly. He could barely hobble up and down the court. Eagletown defeated the Panthers by a very narrow margin. The Eagletown team appeared embarrassed that a black school had given them such a tough game. I suppose had Dunbar beat them they would have been totally devastated. Comments were heard from the Eagletown players after the game to the effect "they played us close, but that was only because they did not have all black players".

Mr. Garfield Johnson, Dunbar's coach, said these comments were in reference to the fact that President, Jr. and Sidney Carter were fair-skinned African Americans and Eagletown players thought they were not black.

Because Dunbar lost by only a few points, it is certain that had President been able to play he would have scored 10 or 15 points at a minimum, giving Dunbar the victory.

Walter Trotter, Terry Franklin, and President Carter, Jr. were outstanding basketball players and each should have been recognized as "All State" players. Each averaged 25 to 30 point scoring averages throughout each basketball season. President Carter went on to play college basketball for Eastern State College at Wilburton coached by Mark Winters. His teams at Eastern State College participated both years in the National Junior College Athletic Association (NJCAA) finals at Hutchinson, Kansas. Later, President, Jr. transferred to Central State University in Edmond where he again played for Coach Mark Winters.

Lady Panther Basketball

The Panthers also fielded creditable women's basketball teams throughout its history. Notable women basketball players for the Lady Panthers were Clara Mae Walker, Doris Jean Polk, Christine Lewis, Thelmarie Lewis, Elmarene Warner, and Bobby Faye Cubit. Not pictured are Ruby Lee Carter, Ina Mae Richards, Elmer Jane Warner, Roberta Spigner, and Lillie Bell Duckett.

Dunbar's last girls' basketball team was in 1964. The team included Bobby L. Savage, Ruth Lewis McPowell, Della Cooper Ivory, Patricia Carter Hearne, Mary Hill Hawkins, Laura Ruth Lewis, Bonnie Lewis, and Allie Lewis. All the girl's teams were coached by Mrs. Catherine Spigner.

Lady Panthers last basketball team.

Football

Sam Young, Cleon Hill, Clarence Radford, Charles Kennybrew, Ike and Elmer Maddock, Jimmy Lee Love, J. D. Garrett, Charles Burris, Hardy Dickerson, and Elijah Burris, among others, were standouts in football. Dunbar teams won consecutive back to back State Championships defeating Frederick in 1951 for the championship and defeating Stillwater in 1952 for the State Championship prize. Due to segregation, Dunbar was restricted to playing only other black schools. Professor Spigner, the coach of the 1951 and 1952 teams adamantly boasted that his team could have beaten any team, white or black, in the state at that time. It has been reported that Professor Spigner even challenged Langston University to a game against his Panthers,

One of Dunbar's early rugged football teams.

which obviously never happened. He even offered to play Oklahoma City's Douglass High School, an all-black 5A school.

Fierce competition existed even during the segregated years when the Dunbar Panthers of Broken Bow played Booker T. Washington Wild Cats of Idabel. A common saying between the two schools was, "you may win the game but you'll lose the fight afterwards." No serious incidents ever came about as the two schools competed; however, there was always a lot of "trash talking" before and after each game. It has been said that Dunbar students in Broken Bow did not care if they lost all their games during the season as long as they beat Idabel. This feeling was mutual for Idabel students as well. Fierce competition still exists even today between the Broken Bow and Idabel athletic programs.

1962 Dunbar High School football team and Homecoming Court.

It is the game that residents from both towns look forward to with great expectations for a win. Over the past few years, Broken Bow has dominated the series.

    Although Dunbar was poorly funded, the black community solidly supported its athletic teams. An avid supporter and follower of all Dunbar teams was President

SPORTS 147

Carter, Sr. He never missed a game, home or away. Perhaps not well known to the public, it has been reported that President Carter paid for the entire football team's first set of new uniforms.

Dunbar took a hiatus from football after 1958 and did not field another football team until the 1962-1963 season. Dunbar High School played its home football games in the historic Broken Bow Memorial Stadium built in the 1930s by the Works Progress Administration (WPA). Built primarily of concrete and native rock, Memorial Stadium is one of the oldest and largest high school stadiums in the State of Oklahoma.

Dunbar High School fielded its last football team during the 1963-1964 school year.

Because this book is intended to cover events and activities up to 1965 or prior to integration, not much is mentioned about two of Broken Bow's greatest black athletes. Larry Taylor and LeVell Hill were two of the best athletes in the state of Oklahoma in the mid-sixties. They were the first black athletes to play for the Broken Bow Savages High School. Both were outstanding in football and track and field. It has been said that with these two athletes could win any competition singlehanded. The saying proved true because these two athletes promptly led Broken Bow to its first appearance in a football state championship game. The Savages lost to the Clinton Red Tornados in 1965; however, the next year Larry Taylor and LeVell Hill led the Broken Bow Savages to its first State Track Championship.

Their accomplishments are thoroughly chronicled in the book *Broken Bow: The First Century* authored by accomplished and famed writer Bob Burke, another talented

Broken Bow native.

Larry Taylor entered the United States Marine Corps after graduation. He was killed in Vietnam in 1968. LeVell Hill accepted a football scholarship to Langston University where he was a standout. He also played Professional Football for a short period of time.

Dunbar Bands

Though not viewed as a sport, Dunbar assembled a marching and concert band over the years. As previously referenced, several teachers directed the Panther Bands including Jimmy Carter, A. D. Bennett, Jr., George Shaver, B. N. Brown, and Herman Stewart. Annual music concerts were held in early spring at various schools. The concerts consisted of bands from Broken Bow, Idabel, Hugo, and Paris, Texas, among other schools. During the early years, the Dunbar Band was marginal at best and did not compete well against the other schools; however, Dunbar assembled its most renowned band under the direction of Herman Stewart, a native son of Broken Bow and a Dunbar graduate. Stewart completed his music degree at Langston University with honors. He returned to Broken Bow as Dunbar's band director in the early sixties. Under his direction, instead of performing traditional basic compositions, he introduced more difficult arrangements such as *CC Trocadera, Mozart's*

Festival, John Phillip Sousa's *Washington Post*, and *El Capitan Marches*. The band developed and produced a sound that rivaled much larger bands even though its membership was less than fifty students.

Gibbons High School in Paris, Texas set the standards for black school bands at most of the concerts and was looked upon as having a premier band, setting the benchmark for the best band in the region during this time. Their band was approximately 80 to 90 members strong and included instruments such as oboes, flutes, xylophones, and timpani kettledrum percussions. These were instruments Dunbar band students had never heard of; however upon the arrival of Stewart, and under his direction and leadership, even the Paris, Texas band took note of the new sound the Dunbar band produced. *"Congratulations Mr. Stewart. You made everyone take note of us."*

Chorus

Dunbar High School also annually assembled a chorus under the direction of B N. Brown, among other directors. Hazel Alford served as the pianist for the chorus. Like the band, the chorus also competed yearly in choir competitions. The chorus competed quite well against other schools. Songs such as *Madame Jeanette, Swing Low Sweet Chario, The Navajo Trail, Dry Bones, Sweet Adeline* and *When the Deep Purple Fall* were regularly performed. Outstanding singers in the chorus were Clarence Radford, Edward Garrett, Cleon Hill, and Sonny Hamilton, Later, Val Gene Golston, Robert Lee Polk, Burnell Garrett, Olivia Jordan, Robbie Parker, Dorothy Ann Burris, Peggy Barr, and Laureen Alford were noted singers in the Dunbar Chorus.

SCHOOL SONG

There is a place we love so dear
Its name will ever ring in revere
It's Dunbar High School that we love
Just one more step and there's heaven above
Dunbar High our Alma mater
Pleasant memories never forgot
Heaven and earth they sons and daughter
All their glory is thy light
Love and loyalty forever is our pledge to thee

SECOND STANZA

Though we may part when school is done
We'll cherish memories days of fun
And when our High School days are through
These are words we'll always say
Dunbar High our Alma mater

Pleasant memories never forgot
Heaven and earth thy sons and daughters
All their glory is thy light
Love and loyalty forever is our pledge to thee

THIRD STANZA

And when the setting sun shall vanish
Stand beside us; and guide us
Through the night with a light from above
Dunbar High our Alma mater

Pleasant memories never forgot
Heaven and earth thy sons and daughters
Will thy blessing be
Love and loyalty forever is our pledge to thee

TRAUMATIC EVENTS THAT OCCURRED INVOLVING DUNBAR STUDENTS

During the time period this writing covers, Dunbar students encountered several traumatic or tragic events.

- Clarence "C Baby" Reynolds, Jr. almost lost his life when he was severely burned at the Barber Shop where he worked in Broken Bow.
- During the time that Dunbar School was being renovated, students attended Macedonia Church for classes. As a student attending Macedonia, Mertha Bell Butler was hit by a car as she ran across the street chasing a ball during recess.
- As a student attending Macedonia, William Kennybrew was struck in the head by a large rock that he had thrown up into a tree to dislodge a football that had become stuck. While concentrating on the football he was trying to dislodge, he forgot about the rock he had just thrown up into the tree. The large rock came back down and caused a huge gash in his forehead that required numerous stitches to close.
- In the summer of 1960, at the age of 16, Kenneth Stuart drowned while swimming in a pond behind Jack Lane's home. Wilber Jefferson "Sonny" Warner, Donnell Williams, Martin "M. J." Warner, and Opal Broussard, all Dunbar students, were swimming in the pond that day. Sonny made several attempts to save Kenneth after he submerged by diving under the water where Kenneth had gone down. Unfortunately, Sonny was unable to rescue Kenneth. Later that afternoon the pond was dragged to locate Kenneth's body.
- During recess, while playing softball, President Carter, Jr. was accidentally struck in the face by a bat swung by

Vernell Ramsey. The impact was so forceful it broke the jaw of President, Jr. His jaw was wired shut for several weeks.

SUMMARY

It would be a misrepresentation of Broken Bow, its black citizens, and Dunbar High School to say that there were no difficult times during the era this writing encompasses. There certainly were challenges for the town of Broken Bow, its black citizens, the churches, the communities, and the Dunbar School, especially during the "dust bowl years", a phenomenon that caused severe drought coupled with decades of extensive farming without crop rotation, cover crops, or other techniques to prevent soil erosion.

Additionally, the Great Depression, originating in the United States, began with the fall of stock prices and the ultimate crash of the market on October 29, 1929, known as Black Tuesday. This major market crash quickly spread to almost every country in the world. The whole nation felt the travails of these events. Yet, in spite of these calamities the town of Broken Bow, its black citizens, the communities, the churches, and Dunbar survived.

Numerous black citizens who persisted and survived the aforementioned events have greatly contributed to the rich storied history of the town of Broken Bow.

The Broken Bow schools were integrated in 1965. The Dunbar High School facility became Eastside Junior High School. History records the process of integration occurred smoothly without any adversity, thanks to Superintendent Rector Johnson, Broken Bow High School Principal Pierce

Martin, his administrative staff, and black citizens such as Gertrude Lewis, Willie Jordan, Sr., Professor Garfield Johnson, Martin Lewis, and Curtis Cantley.

This writing has merely been an attempt to highlight a few of the lives and events of black citizens of Broken Bow from the time of incorporation in 1910 up to the year of integration in 1965. Many outstanding black citizens and athletes after integration in 1965 contributed to making Broken Bow the town it is today.

Much of Broken Bow's history after 1965 is vividly documented in the outstanding book entitled *Broken Bow: The First Century*, authored by Bob Burke, Harriet Burris Martin, Kenneth Hamilton, and Paulette LaGasse. Their writings played a great part in inspiring me to write this book.

I hope that everyone who reads this book develops a clearer understanding of the town of Broken Bow; its beginning, the progress it has made, and a greater appreciation for the black communities in the great city of Broken Bow as it exists today. If you have never visited the town of Broken Bow, I would encourage you to do so. It is a wonderful town and a place I will always remember as home.

BIBLIOGRAPHY

Oklahoma Historical Society's *Encyclopedia of Oklahoma Culture*

Wikipedia, the free Encyclopedia

Burke, Bob. *Broken Bow: The First Century*

Guest, Edgar A. . "Sermons We See", *the Light of Faith*, The Reilly & Lee Company, Chicago, 1926.

Big Springs Daily Herald

INDEX

$64,000 Question 26
77 Sunset Strip 26

A

Adam, Lyord
Alford, Clyde 35
Alford, Hazel M. 64, 74, 150
Alford, Laureen 90, 93, 99, 150
Alfred Hitchcock Presents 26
American Bandstand 26
American Legion Post 297 30
Amos 'n Andy 26
Amos, Crossie Mae *see* Crossie Mae Kennybrew
Amos, Flossie Mae *see* Flossie Mae Carter
Anderson family 34
Anderson, E.D. 65
Anderson, Mrs. E. D. 65
Annie V 47
Arnold, Lula 34
Arnold, Maye Helen *see* Maye Helen Leffall
Ashdown, AR 140
Atkinson family 35, 78
Atkinson, Alcleata 89-92
Atkinson, Rowena *see* Rowena Lewis
Atoka, OK 141
Aunt Verdie *see* Verdie Lewis
Austin, Lewis 101
"Away in a Manger" 49

B

Bagsby, Pearl 35
Baker, Dr. _____ 18
Banks, Mr. _____ 54
Barber, Elmo 34

Barr, Peggy 88, 150
Barr, Prema Lee 101
Barr, Rosella 35, 64, 71, 91
Beavers Bend State Park 13-14, 76
Beggs, OK 141
Bell, Johnnie 49
Benford, Ruby 35
Bennett, A. D. 35, 54, 149
Bennett, L. D., Jr. 65
Bernice, LA 140
Bethel, OK 30
Bethlehem Baptist Church 48
Big Springs Daily Herald 75
Big Springs, TX 75
Billie, Clarence 97
Bizzell, Elizabeth 49, 70
Bizzell, Emmitt, Jr. 6, 34, 49
Bizzell, Leola 49, 70
Bizzell, Maxine *see* Maxine Bizzell Golston
Bizzell, Ralph 6, 49
Bizzell, Rosetta 49, 86, 91
Bizzell, Ruthel 49, 98
Bizzell, Willie M. 91
Blakely, OK 36
Bonham, TX 141
Booker family 35
Booker T. Washington High School 146
Booker, Rodester 86, 90-91
Bostic, Maxcine Lewis 102, 109, 116, 121, 128
Boswell, OK 56, 141
Brewer, Jack 26, 34, 40
Brewer, Levolia 40
Broken Bow City Hall 23
Broken Bow Lake 14

Broken Bow Memorial Stadium 30, 148
Broken Bow, NB 11
Broken Bow: The First Century 32, 148, 154
Broussard, Alene 34
Broussard, Cleo 68, 115, 122
Broussard, Frank 34
Broussard, Ivory 68
Broussard, James Edward 29, 68, 98
Broussard, James, Sr. 33
Broussard, Katy 68
Broussard, Kenneth 20, 68
Broussard, Lillie Bell Duckett 48, 78, 91, 98, 110, 119, 144
Broussard, Lonzo 68
Broussard, Mary 68
Broussard, Opal 68, 152
Broussard, Vinnie Mae 68
Brown, B. N. 65, 149-150
Brown, LaVern 67
Brown, O. D. 96-97
Burke, Bob 32, 148, 154
Burrell, Johnnie Mae Carter 110, 115, 119, 129
Burris, Alexander "Zanders" 34
Burris, James "Pip" 5,
Burris, Alice 75
Burris, Anna Mae
Burris, Arthel 34, 54, 98
Burris, Beatrice 70
Burris, Bertha Lena 50
Burris, Calvin 34, 49
Burris, Charles 6, 145
Burris, Charlie 6, 67
Burris, Clarence 5
Burris, Cornell 68, 132
Burris, Donald 6, 122, 126
Burris, Dorothy Ann 68, 88, 150

Burris, Dorothy Mae *see* Dorothy Mae Carter
Burris, Earl 34
Burris, Edith 68
Burris, Elijah 6, 78, 98, 145
Burris, Frank 96
Burris, G. B. 6
Burris, Harrison 34
Burris, Hattie 34
Burris, Hickman 5, 34
Burris, Isaac 49
Burris, James "Pip" 5, 34, 50, 97
Burris, Jodie 34, 48, 55
Burris, Juliann 49
Burris, Mae Anna 67
Burris, Mary 34, 68, 97
Burris, Maryliza 34
Burris, Ola Mae 68, 97
Burris, Parker 34
Burris, Pearl 98
Burris, Pinky 48
Burris, Rastus "Bo Do" 5, 34, 50, 97
Burris, Ray 14, 67, 101
Burris, Robert 5
Burris, Roberta 18, 48
Burris, Simon 35, 54
Burris, Ulysses 78
Burris, Van 78
Burris, Willie Isaac 78, 98
Butler, Charles Henry 5, 34, 103, 111, 116, 118, 121, 129
Butler, Claretha *see* Claretha Butler Cubit
Butler, Dorothy 91
Butler, Herman 34
Butler, Ivory Lee, Jr. 6, 134, 137
Butler, Ivory Lee, Sr. 34, 55
Butler, Jake 29, 33

Butler, Jeannie 111, 118
Butler, Mary Bell *see* Mary Bell Cooper
Butler, Mertha Bell 152
Butler, W. C. 29, 54

C

Caldwell, James 5
California State University 57
Callaham family 16
Callaham, Jewel 59
Cantley, Curtis 5, 24, 33, 53, 59, 154
Carson, Addie 18, 48
Carson, CA 57
Carson, Ester 34
Carson, Otis 34, 48
Carter, Aaron 34, 97
Carter, Barbara 10
Carter, Clifford 5, 26, 54, 68
Carter, Dorothy Mae 98
Carter, Flossie Mae 39, 45, 75
Carter, Frances 55
Carter, Herman 6, 26, 44, 68, 78, 96-98
Carter, James Edward 6, 20, 55, 68, 78, 96, 98, 106
Carter, Jimmy 65, 149
Carter, Johnnie B. 26, 68, 78, 98
Carter, Johnnie Mae *see* Johnnie Mae Carter Burrell
Carter, Lakisha 10
Carter, Mark 10, 108, 111, 113-114, 125, 127, 130-131
Carter, Opalene 40, 46, 68, 78
Carter, Patricia *see* Patricia Hearne
Carter, President, Jr. 6, 10, 20, 78, 98, 105-106, 11, 112, 115-117, 143, 152-153

156   BROKEN BOW'S BLACK COMMUNITIES AND DUNBAR HIGH SCHOOL

Carter, President, Sr. 20, 22-24, 34, 44, 147-148

Carter, Ruby 50, 68, 78, 98-99, 144

Carter, Scarlett *see Scarlett Carter Henderson*

Carter, Sedalia 5

Carter, Sidney, Sr. 6, 10, 78, 88, 96, 98, 101-103, 105-106, 108, 111, 113-114, 119, 124-127, 130-131, 135-136, 139, 143

Carter, Sidney, Jr. 10

Carter, Steve 10

Carter, Tom 34

Cedar Creek Golf Course 14

Central State University 143

Chandler, Granville 61

Chandler, Harold 18, 61

Chandler, Paul 61

Chandler, Rex 61

Chandler, Rex, Jr. 61

Chastain, Dr. _____ 18

Cherry, Earnestine Jordan 32, 41, 43, 61-62, 68, 78, 98

Cherry, Manuel 61, 98

Chief Theater 26-27

Choctaw Lumber Company 11, 32

Choctaw Tribe 11

Ciscero, Willie 33, 68

Civil War 11, 28

Clebit, OK 36

Clinton, OK 148

Colbert, Andrew 6

Colbert, Manuel 6, 34, 100

Colbert, Marylene 99

Colbert, OK 141

Colbert, Rosena 98

Colbert, Thomas 98

Cole, Archie D. "Mr. Ted" 41

Cole, Evelyn Jo 68

Cole, Willie Mae 29, 33, 55

Coleman, Herndon 34

Colgate, OK 142

Committee for Industrial Organization (CIO) 35-36

Cooper, Carlos 78

Cooper, Della *see Della Cooper Ivory*

Cooper, Lonnie 34, 49, 98

Cooper, Mable 35

Cooper, Mary Bell 49, 64, 73, 98

Cooper, Marylyn 78

Cooper, TX 141

Cotton, Opalene Hill 78, 98, 123-124, 130

Cotton, Paula Pillers 101

Cottons, Bill 101

Cottons, Cliff 101

Cottons, James 101

County Barn 36

Craig Fiber Plant 61

Crawford, M. T.

Creed, Bertie 17

Crouse's Dairy Freeze 27

Cubit, Joe Walter "Sugar" 78

Cubit, Ada Bell 92

Cubit, Ardis 55, 68, 78, 98-99, 105, 111-113, 121

Cubit, Betty 139

Cubit, Bobby Faye 78, 86, 144

Cubit, Brenda 112-113, 121

Cubit, Claretha Butler 118, 120, 124

Cubit, Claude Lee 139

Cubit, Genie 26

Cubit, J. W. 68

Cubit, Joe David 34, 78

Cunts, A. Z. "Mose" 26, 68

Cunts, Rosie 33

D

Dairy Queen 27

Dallas, Cleve 29, 33

Dangerfield, TX 141

Davis, Johnny Kate 48

Davis, Louisa Mae 48, 98

Davis, Roy 34, 48, 96

Dean, Jerry 142

Demco 55

DeQueen, AR 30

Dickerson, Hardy Lee 145

Dickersons family 35

Dierks Lumber Company 23, 28, 33, 35-36, 52-53, 61

Dierks, Hans 11, 13

Dierks, Herman 11, 13

Dillahunty, Parthenia Owens 67, 101, 104

Dobney, Dr. _____ 18

Douglass High School 146

Dowell, Jimmy 96

Dragnet 26

Duckett family 34

Duckett, Cecil 68

Duckett, Chonkie 6

Duckett, Clifford 6, 33

Duckett, Donna Faye 68

Duckett, Edna Brown 48

Duckett, Eloise Nelson 101, 108, 119-120, 125, 133-134, 139

Duckett, Harold 6

Duckett, Lillie Bell *see Lillie Bell Broussard*

Duckett, Loren 128

Duckett, Ollie 49-50, 78

Duckett, Ruben 6, 78

Duckett, Sammy 49-50, 78

Duckett, Theresa 49

Dude, Son 33

E

Eagletown 63, 67, 75-76, 97, 142-143

Earnest, Archie 96

Earnest, Curtis 34

Eastern State College 60, 143

Eastside Community Center 100, 104

Eastside Junior High 63, 153

Ebony Gospel Trumpets 50

Echols, Violet M. 65

Ed Sullivan Show, The 26

Edmond, OK 143

El Reno, OK 96

Elder, Emma Lee "Pig" 34, 68

Elder, James 97

Elder, Mary Lee *see Mary Burris*

Elder, Robert 34

Elder, Taylor 33, 43, 68

Encyclopedia of Oklahoma History and Culture 8

F

Food Makers 55

Ford Motor company 20

Foreman, AR 140

Franklin, Terry 143

Frazier, Fezell 68

Frazier, Juanita 68

Frazier, Willie B. 68

Frazier, Willie L., Jr. 6, 68, 88, 110, 116, 119, 122

Frazier, Willie L., Sr. 33

Frederick, OK 141, 145

Friday Night wrestling 26

Fulsom, Caroline

Fulsom, Caroline *see Caroline Reynolds*

Fulsom, W. B. 35

Future Farmers of America (FFA) 72

G

Gable, Austin 34

Gafford, C. L. 48

Galveston, TX 28

Garrett, Annie V. 54

Garrett, Burnell 78, 150

Garrett, Charles 78

Garrett, Edgar 35, 47

Garrett, Edward L. 6, 150

Garrett, J. D. 78, 145

Garrett, Jackie 6, 78

Garrett, Sylvester 78

Garrett, Wilbur D. 6, 78

Gates, Rixie 62, 64

Gems' Café 27

General Electric Hour, The 26

Gibbons High School 150

Gilmore, Abe 33

Givens, John 35

"God Bless America" 75

Goff, Jake 34

Golston, Billie 68

Golston, Charlie 20, 68, 98

Golston, Floyd 33

Golston, Maxine Bizzell 86, 90, 98

Golston, Val Gene 20, 68, 98, 100, 150

Gordon, Homer 26, 35, 50

Graham, T. C. 35

Granger, Gordon 28

Graves, E. D. 48

Gray, Martha 75

Gray, Pearletta 65

Green, James Allen "Bae" 34

Green, John "Dock" 34

Green, Ruby Jewel 121, 123, 127

Guest, Edgar A. 79

Gunsmoke 26

INDEX   157

H

Hackett, Bernice 6, 20, 98, 102-103, 109, 137

Hackett, Eddie Mae 35

Hackett, Sherlean 137-138

Hall, Ray 142

Hall, S.P. 96

Hamilton family 78

Hamilton, Al Q. 35

Hamilton, Bill 6

Hamilton, Kenneth 154

Hamilton, Sonny 150

Hamilton, Winzell 6, 55

Hankins, Daisy 68

Hankins, Landon 68

Hankins, Mozell *see Mozell Hankins Pennington*

Hankins, Odell 68

Hankins, Smith 33

Hankins, Will 34

Harris family 35

Harris, Dunnie 5

Harris, Gene 23, 59

Harris, Mrs. _____ 64

Harris, Walter "Dago" 35

Harrison, Napolean 35

Have Gun Will Travel 26

Hawkins, Mary Hill 101, 123, 131, 144

Hawthorne, Dellie 5

Hearne, Patricia Carter 78, 94, 98, 109, 111, 114-116, 121, 144

Henderson, Johnnie 109, 113-114, 118, 121

Henderson, Scarlett Carter 68, 78, 89-91, 98, 100, 109, 112-114, 118

Hendricks, Runion "Champ" 33, 58-59

Hewitt, Chandler 20; drugstore 20, 27

Hicks, Ray 142

Highway Patrol 26

Hill, Bonnie Mae 78, 86, 89-91, 98, 100

Hill, Cedell 6, 78

Hill, Cleon 6, 78, 145, 150

Hill, Dennis 50, 78, 96

Hill, Leon 78

Hill, LeVell 78, 101, 108, 117-118, 126-127, 129-130, 132, 134, 139, 148-149

Hill, Lilly May *see Lilly May Young*

Hill, Lola 78, 88

Hill, Mary 78, 98

Hill, Mary *see Mary Hill Hawkins*

Hill, Opalene *see Opalene Hill Cotton*

Hill, Ora 78, 88

Hill, Pearl *see Pearl Hill Hunter*

Hill, Sam 34, 55

Hills Chapel 49-50

Hochatown State Park 14

Hodge, Mrs. _____ 64

Hollings, Henry 33

Holly Springs, MS 56

Holmes, W.T. 33, 50

Honey Grove, TX 141

Hope, AR 140

Hough, Joe 20, 23, 59

House, Edward 65, 95

House, Mrs. B. Williams 64

Hughes, Charles 62, 64

Hugo, OK 141, 149

Hunter, Pearl Anna Hill 78, 101, 110, 120, 123, 125

Hutchinson, KS 143

I

I Love Lucy 26

Idabel High School 108

Idabel, OK 51, 54, 56, 58-59, 141, 146, 149

"In the Mood" 30

Irons, Walter 23

Isaac, Opalene 35

Ivory, Della Cooper 56, 78, 93-94, 98, 130, 144

Ivory, Donald 56

J

Jackson National Life Insurance Company 55

Jackson, Edward 106-107, 128, 132, 138-139

Jackson, Mary Vernell Johnson 78, 98, 108, 117, 122, 134-138

Jewel, Ruby *see Ruby Jewel Green*

Johnson family 78

Johnson, Daisy Lewis 102-103, 110, 129

Johnson, Garfield 143, 154

Johnson, Garnetta *see Garnetta Johnson Sweet*

Johnson, Lonnie 6

Johnson, Mary 90, 93

Johnson, Rector 153

Jolly Inn 54

Jones, Tee Bo 23

Jordan, Bradley 61

Jordan, Earnestine *see Earnestine Cherry*

Jordan, Flossie Mae *see Flossie Mae Carter*

Jordan, John 6, 20, 61, 99

Jordan, Michael 20, 61

Jordan, Mildred Pickens 36, 98

Jordan, Narvel 43

Jordan, Olivia 68, 98-99, 150

Jordan, Willie Lee Sr. 5, 35, 38, 60-61, 68, 78, 98, 154

Jordan, Willie Lee, Jr. 20, 60-61, 68, 101

Juneteenth 28, 30

K

KBEL Radio 51

Kellum, Billy J. 6

Kennon, _____ 63-64

Kennybrew, Carl 50, 78

Kennybrew, Charles 50, 78, 98, 101, 106-107, 118-119, 123, 125, 133-134, 137-138, 145

Kennybrew, Christine 112, 117, 123, 133, 137-138

Kennybrew, Crossie Mae 39, 47

Kennybrew, Gloria 117, 123, 132

Kennybrew, Harold 78, 130

Kennybrew, Marvin 39

Kennybrew, Neely 48

Kennybrew, Pearly Mae 78

Kennybrew, Roy 34, 48

Kennybrew, Theodis 6, 55, 78, 107, 112, 114, 117-118, 123, 126, 131-132

Kennybrew, William 78, 96, 98, 103, 131, 135-136, 152

Kennybrew, Wilma Jean 78

Kiamichi Mountains 11

Kiamichi Technical Center 56

King, Bee 33, 53

King, Big Boy 29

King, Catherine 43, 53-54

King, Elzie Lee 23, 46, 68

King, John 34

King, Minnie Jewel 68

King, Willie Lee 68

Korean Conflict 5-6

L

Lacy, Leon 95

LaGasse, Paulette 154

Lane Industry 13

Lane, Clarence 23, 30

Lane, Jack 20, 152

Lane's Motor Company 30

Langston University 60, 94, 145, 149

Langston, OK 60

Leffall, Maye Helen 48, 56, 98, 113

Leffall, Reginald Mack, III 57

Lewis, Adell, Jr. 6, 78

Lewis, Adell, Sr. 34, 49, 54, 62, 97

Lewis, Allie 144

Lewis, Anna Faye 56, 78, 89, 98, 100

Lewis, Anna Kay 67

Lewis, Bertha Mae 40, 98

Lewis, Bertie Mae 56, 92

Lewis, Bonnie 144

Lewis, Bryant 34, 49, 56, 96

Lewis, Carl 67

Lewis, Charles Jr. 6, 90

Lewis, Charles, Sr. 34

Lewis, Christine *see Christine Lewis Ratcliff*

Lewis, Clarence, Sr. 6, 67, 76, 98

Lewis, Daisy *see Daisy Johnson*

Lewis, Delcia 49, 97

Lewis, Dixie Jo 90-91

Lewis, Garland 78

Lewis, Gary Grant 67, 76

Lewis, Gertrude 49, 56, 62, 64, 73-74, 78, 98, 101, 105, 107, 154

Lewis, Isaiah 6, 107, 114, 118, 127, 131

Lewis, J'Rae 105, 107

Lewis, Julius 24, 114

Lewis, L. C. 78

Lewis, L. D. 6, 78

Lewis, L. W., Jr. 20

Lewis, L.W., Sr. 34
Lewis, Laura Ruth 67, 93, 144
Lewis, Louise 35
Lewis, Martin 5, 34, 49, 59, 96, 98, 154
Lewis, Mary Lou 56, 91
Lewis, Maxcine see Maxcine Lewis Bostic
Lewis, Roosevelt "Pluck" 34, 55
Lewis, Rosetta 67, 99
Lewis, Rowena 90, 98
Lewis, Roxanne 35
Lewis, Rueben Dale 67
Lewis, Ruth see Ruth Lewis McPowell
Lewis, Thelmarie see Thelmarie Lewis Sykes
Lewis, Tomycine 56, 93
Lewis, Verdie 18, 34
Lewis, Walter 6, 78
Lewis, Willie "W. L." 6, 20, 30, 78
Light of Faith, The 79
Lincoln, Abraham 28
Little Rascals, The 26
Locksburg, AR 140
Long Beach Bible College 57
Longview, TX 55
Los Angeles City College 57
Los Angeles County, CA 57
Los Angeles Unified School District 55
Los Angeles, CA 55, 57
Love, Jimmy Lee 6, 98, 145
Lucas, TX 101
Lucy Ann, Ms. 34
Lukfata 17, 25, 28, 33-34, 63, 96
Lyord, Adam 33

M

Macedonia Baptist Church 48, 104, 152
Maddock family 34
Maddock, Elmer 6, 77-78, 145
Maddock, Ike 6, 55, 77-78, 96, 105, 111, 115-116, 128-129, 131, 135-136, 145
Majors, Reverend 34, 48
Marrow, Violet Echols 34
Martin, Harriet Burris 154
Martin, Pierce 153-154
McAlester, OK 141
McCurtain County, OK 11, 14-15, 21, 23, 36, 58, 140
McDonald, C. T. 18
McGuatha, Joyce 108
McKissic, Rev. _____ 49
McPowell, Ruth Lewis 56, 78, 96-98, 101, 144
Meacham, Allen 34, 49-50
Melissa, Mrs. _____ 34
Mendelssohn, Feliz 74
Mighty Clouds of Joy 51
Miles, Ollie Bessie 33, 68
Mills, Cleve 70
Mills, V. L. 53
Mineral Springs, AR 140
Missouri City, TX 56
Moore, Riley 20
Morgan, Bobby 101, 108, 125
Morren, Ortho 17
Morris, Florene 91, 121, 123, 127
Moses, Neal 35
Mountain Fork River 14
Mullins, G. C. 18

N

Naples, TX 141
National Junior College Athletic Association (NJCAA) 143
Nelson, Eloise see *Eloise Duckett*
Nelson, Joyce 126-127
New Addition 28, 33, 35, 38, 48, 54, 56, 62, 64
New Farmers of America (NFA) 71
New Homemakers of America (NHA) 71
Nobles, J. S. 48

O

"Oh Come All Ye Faithful" 49
"Oh Little Town of Bethlehem" 49
Oklahoma Blood Institute 56
Oklahoma City, OK 55-56, 61, 146
Oklahoma Historical Society 10
Okmulgee, OK 56, 141
Oscar's Restaurants 55
Owens, Clyde 67
Owens, Jessie Lee 67
Owens, Parthenia see *Parthenia Owens Dillahunty*

P

Pace, _____ 20
Paris, TX 141, 149-150
Parker, Earnest 67
Parker, Gloria 67, 98
Parker, Magdaline 67
Parker, Robbie 67, 98, 150
Parks, Odelia 35
Pasture 32
Paxston, Jessie 34
Payne, Charles 98
Pennington, Clarence "C. J.", Jr. 6, 38, 68, 78
Pennington, Clarence, Sr. 33, 42, 97
Pennington, Credell 68
Pennington, Maybell 68
Pennington, Mozell Hankins 68, 97
Pettis, Corine 110, 113, 115, 119, 124, 136
Pickens, Mildred see *Mildred Pickens Jordan*
Pillers, Paula see *Paula Pillers Cotton*
Pine Park 48
Plano, TX 55
Playhouse 90 26
Pleasant Valley 8, 17, 20, 22-23, 25, 28, 33-34, 48-50, 54, 56, 62-64, 96
Pledge of Allegiance 75
Pole Yard 68
Polk, Chaney 35
Polk, Doris 67, 144
Polk, Ike 67, 96
Polk, Leon 67
Polk, Robert Lee 150
"Pomp and Circumstance" 74
Portland, OR 55
Powderly, TX 100, 141
Prudential Corporation 55

Q

Quarters 23-25, 28, 32-35, 48, 53, 67-68

R

Radford, Clarence 6, 78, 145, 150
Radford, Nora 35
Ramsey, Allen 78
Ramsey, I. D. 78
Ramsey, Jessie Mae Warren 106
Ramsey, Jewel 35
Ramsey, Vernell 6, 56, 78, 98, 101, 108, 119, 125, 132, 135, 138, 153
Ratcliff, Christine Lewis 56, 144
Rattan, OK 142
Releford, Patricia 35
Reynolds, Caroline 98
Reynolds, Clarence "C Baby", Jr. 34, 152
Reynolds, Martha 75
Reynolds, Willie Lee 96, 98
Richard, Earnest 34
Richard, Lycurgus 34
Richards, Cecil 101, 113, 121, 129
Richards, Christina "Feddie" 49
Richards, Erma 49
Richards, Ina Mae 49, 144
Richards, Lucretia 62, 64
Richards, M. C. 6
Richards, Maureen 90, 100
Richards, McCurtain 34
Richards, Paul 6, 88, 96, 99
Richards, Pearl 49
Richards, Robert
Richards, Roman 34
Richards, William L. 34, 49
Riverside High School 100-103, 107-108
Roark, Dr. _____ 18
Rose, Willie 34
Rust College 56

S

San Diego, CA 55, 61
Sapulpa, OK 141
Savage, Bobby L. 68, 144
Savage, Pearl 75
Savage, Phil 29, 33
Sears 56
"Sermons We See" 79

Shaver, George 64, 88, 149

Shaver, Irma Anderson 65, 86

Sherrill, Dr. _____ 18

Shomore family 35

Shoulders, Jim 30

Shuford, Dr. _____ 18

"Silent Night" 49

Simmons, Ora 101

Sitoka, AR 140

Skeens, Don 23

Smith, Alice Faye *see* Alice Faye Smith Warner

Smith, Linda Faye 129

Smith, Sid 33, 45, 54

Solar Turbine and Engines Corporation 61

Spigner, Catherine 64, 72, 144

Spigner, Geneva 64

Spigner, Nathaniel 70

Spigner, Reedy Mack "R. M.", Sr. 35, 55, 63-64, 70, 100, 145

Spigner, Reedy Macque, Jr. 55, 78, 93, 98, 101, 132-138

Spigner, Roberta 144

Spiritual Five 50

Spotwood 142

Spray Pond 35

St. John's Baptist 48

Stafford, Ola Faye 67, 120, 128

Stewart, Herman 65, 108, 149

Stewart, Snowball 23

Stiles, Robert 12

Stillwater, OK 141, 145

Stuart, Charlie Ray 35

Stuart, Kenneth 152

Stuart, L.C. 35

Superman 26

Sweet, Garnetta Johnson 124, 133

Sykes, Benny J. 78

Sykes, Clennon 78

Sykes, Eddie 6, 68, 96, 98

Sykes, James 6

Sykes, Lennon 6

Sykes, LeVester 78, 86, 98

Sykes, Odell 68

Sykes, Othell 68

Sykes, Thelmarie 67, 98

Sykes, Willie Lee 26, 68

Sykes, Zeola 33

T

Tabernacle of Faith Baptist Church 57

Tate, Willie Mae 35, 75

Taugher, Tim 75

Taylor, Hood 35

Taylor, Larry 6, 148-149

Texas, Oklahoma and Eastern Railroad 11

"The First Noel" 49

Thomas, Charlyne *see* Charlyne Wysinger

Thompson, Curtis 101, 108, 122

TIME Magazine 28

Touchstone, M.L. 24

Touchstone, R. G. 24

Trotter, Consuelo 119, 122-123, 125, 136, 138

Trotter, Walter 68, 112, 115, 122-123, 125-126, 136-138, 143

True Sign 34

Turner, Red 34

Twilight Zone, The 26

Tyson Industries 13, 60

U

United States Corps of Engineers 14

United States Department of Agriculture (USDA) 36

United States Marine Corps 149

University of California at Los Angeles 57

University of Southern California 57

V

Vacation Bible School 50

Valentine, Hattie 51

Valliant, OK 142

Valliant, OK 56

Vernell, Mary *see* Mary Vernell Johnson Jackson

Vietnam 5-6

W

Wagoner, OK 141

Walker, Clara Mae 144

Walker, Jake 34, 55

Walker, Jyles 96

Walker, Pearl *see* Pearl Burris

Walker, Rosa Mae 90

"War March of the Priest" 74

Warner, Alice Faye Smith 67, 103, 120, 128

Warner, Elmarene 68, 144

Warner, Elmer Jane 144

Warner, Elsie Mae 67

Warner, Lurene 34

Warner, Martin "M. J." 68, 88, 99, 105-107, 152

Warner, Ola Mae *see* Ola Mae Burris

Warner, Wilber Jefferson 68, 131, 134, 138, 152

Warren, Clark G. 6, 105-106, 113, 130

Warren, Jessie Mae *see* Jessie Mae Warren Ramsey

Washington, AR 140

Washington, James 101

Watonga, OK 141

Westbrook, Credell 5

Westbrook, Nora 33

Weyerhaeuser Company 13

Whatley, Hardy, Jr. 30

Wheeler, G. W. 35

Wheeler, Otis 35

Wheeler, Walter 6

Wheeler, Webster, Jr. 6

Wheeler, Webster, Sr. 35

White, Berda 18

White, Ollie 34

Whittaker, Dr. _____ 18

Whitten, _____ 20

Wichita, KS 56

Wilburton, OK 60, 143

Williams, LeVan 6

Williams, A. W.

Williams, Bee

Williams, Clint, Jr.

Williams, Clint, Sr. 34, 55, 70

Williams, Cora 35

Williams, Dave 68

Williams, Donnell 152

Williams, Elesta 109

Williams, Fannie 64, 72

Williams, H. O. 35

Williams, Larry 6

Williams, LeVan 6

Wilson family 35

Wilson, Bell 33

Wilson, Shelby 103

Wimbley, Charles 67

Wimbley, Floyd 67

Wimbley, Helen 67

Wimbley, Larkin 23, 50, 67

Wimbley, Virginia 67

Winn, Mrs. _____ 61

Winship family 35

Winters, Mark 143

Wiseman, Arma G. 6, 35

Woods, Charlie 99

Woods, Janie 99

Workman, Roxanna 70

Works Progress Administration (WPA) 148

World War II 5

Wright City, OK 36, 142

Wysinger, Charlyne Thomas 93, 136

Y

Young, Henry 35

Young, Lilly May 29, 98

Young, Sam "S. C.", Jr. 26, 35, 96, 145

Young, Sam, Sr. 29, 35, 98

Z

Zanders, _____ 48

AUTOGRAPHS